Suddenly
You Are Nobody

Suddenly You Are Nobody

VERMONT REFUGEES TELL THEIR STORIES

JARED GANGE

Portrait photography by Katie Figura

HUNTINGTON GRAPHICS
Burlington, Vermont

Published by Huntington Graphics, P.O. Box 373, Burlington, VT 05402

Designed by Andrea Gray
Portrait Photography by Katie Figura
Maps by John Hadden, Resting Lion Studio

ISBN 978-1-886064-53-9

First edition

Printed by Four Colour Print Group, Louisville, Kentucky

Cover photo: Sahela border crossing between Syria and Iraq, September 2013
Photo credit: Christian Jepsen, Norwegian Refugee Council

You live normal life.
Suddenly you are nobody.
Yesterday everybody knows you, knows about you.
Next day you are no one. You are low, below low.

— SLAVOJKA AVDIBEGOVIC
Refugee from Bosnia

You own a house or rent an apartment.
You live with your family or by yourself.
You wake in the morning and drink your coffee or tea.
You drive a car or a motorbike, or perhaps you take the bus.
You go out at night and flirt and date.
You live in a small town or big city,
although maybe you are in the countryside.
You have hopes, dreams and expectations.
You take your humanity for granted.
You keep believing you are human even when the catastrophe
arrives and renders you homeless.
Your town or city or countryside is in ruins.
You try to make it to the border.
Only then, hoping to leave, or making it across the border,
do you understand that those who live on the other side
do not see you as human at all.

— VIET THANH NGUYEN, VIETNAM
Author of *The Sympathizer*,
Pulitzer Prize winner

The world in which you were born is just one model of reality.
Other cultures are not failed attempts at being you;
they are unique manifestations of the human spirit.

— WADE DAVIS
Author, ethnobotanist,
National Geographic Explorer-in-Residence

CONTENTS

FOREWORD

We, who arrive as immigrants and refugees in this country, often bring nothing with us but our memories and stories. As the title of this absorbing and moving collection suggests, we find that suddenly we are nobody. No one knows our story. We are seen as threatening interlopers who need to be sent back to where we came from. More often than not, this view is based on ignorance: a lack of understanding of our circumstances. We are here because we can't go back; the bridge has been burned, our homes no longer safe places where we can thrive. Unwelcome adds salt on the wound of our many losses. Over and above losing everything, we are faced with the challenges of being misunderstood and rejected.

The situation I describe above was that of my own family in 1960 when we fled the Dominican Republic as political refugees. My father had been a member of an underground movement against the 31-year dictatorship and his particular group had been infiltrated by the secret police. He was on the point of being arrested and disappeared—a fate that befell other members of our family who were not as lucky. We escaped to New York City, each with a small suitcase of our belongings, believing in the promise of Lady Liberty, that we had arrived in the land of welcome and opportunity, of freedom and belonging.

That was not to be, not right away, anyhow. Like many of the refugees and immigrants whose stories are collected here, we endured years of struggle, persistence, hard work. But over time what I found was that if I told our story well, people were likely to listen, and their view of us as "other" or threatening shifted. Stories allow us to become the other by putting us in someone else's experience. Reading, we exercise the muscles of the imagination, the same muscles we use in feeling compassion and in being compelled towards social justice activism. We come out of a story that has engaged and moved us as a slightly different person than the one who began reading. Whitman, the quintessential American poet, knew this when he wrote:

I celebrate myself and sing myself,
and what I assume you shall assume
for every atom belonging to me as good belongs to you.

We belong to each other. This is the truest American anthem I know, an affirmation of the DNA that holds us together in a democracy based on equality and diversity.

Jared Gange understands this and he has facilitated the storytelling of a diverse and inspiring group of new fellow Americans gathered here. Like any good storyteller, he puts their arrival in context so that we learn not just about these individuals but about the larger world beyond our borders. Again and again we are moved by their plight as they face what seem insurmountable odds. We are filled with awe and admiration for their resilience and hope, their hard work and contributions to our communities.

When I first arrived in Vermont in the early eighties, my Latino friends and familia used to joke that I had moved to the "Latino compromised state of Vermont." Back then, the lack of diversity exacerbated the feeling of not belonging, of being in the margins. But however cold the winters, Vermonters proved to be a warm-hearted and welcoming sort. Now after almost four decades living in Vermont, it feels like home. More so because of the increasing diversity of our population as new immigrants join our state, infusing it with their energy, dreams, hard work, and talents.

In these times of divisive rhetoric and draconian measures against refugees, *Suddenly You Are Nobody* provides the antidote of understanding, compassion, and rich storytelling. Here we have a diversity of stories—for there is the danger of a single story, othering the other once again in a restrictive stereotype; here we have exemplars of the values we often celebrate when we talk about what makes America great: resilience, resourcefulness, hard work. Reading it you will feel heartened and inspired by these new fellow Americans who have rolled up their sleeves and stretched out their hands, not for handouts as the xenophobic diatribes claim, but to help us build a better Vermont, a better country, and a better world. They are not nobodies, they are you and me—the best we all can aspire to be.

— Julia Alvarez, author of
How the García Girls Lost Their Accents,
Return to Sender, Something to Declare,
among other titles.
March 2019

Introduction

What is a refugee? A refugee is a person who has been forced from his or her country—usually to a neighboring country—and is afraid or unable to return. The primary causes are war, ethnic persecution, religious intolerance, drought and famine. Some have been driven at gunpoint from home and country, after being forced to sign papers indicating they are leaving of their own free will; others have fled their burning homes in the middle of the night, losing everything; and some have been forced to witness unspeakable acts inflicted on their parents, their spouses or their children. In other words, they flee for reasons that would cause any rational person to flee. Robert Achinda, a refugee from the Democratic Republic of Congo, gives an idea of the desperation of the moment when recalling his 30-mile crossing of storm-prone Lake Tanganyika, in a flimsy boat, to safety in Tanzania: *You stay, you die. You cross, maybe you die, maybe you live: you decide!*

Another aspect of the plight of refugees who have been resettled in another country is that many, if not most, have little choice where they will be sent. This is not to imply that those who are resettled here in Vermont or other locations in the U.S. did not want to come here or are ungrateful to have been sent here, but once you have fled your home country and

Yazidi girl in a refugee camp in northern Iraq, 2014. ISIS attempted to exterminate the entire Yazidi population.

become a refugee, you have very little control over your fate. It is a sad fact that today there are millions in refugee camps in Kenya, Lebanon, Turkey and Bangladesh—to name a few countries with large refugee populations—who do not know what the future holds for them. This uprooting, this abrupt end of one's normal existence and the lack of control over one's destiny is expressed by local resident Suhad Murad: *We originally from Iraq. We live all our lives in Iraq. We never plan to come here or anywhere.*

The United States spends more than any other nation on foreign development aid, and much of this is in response to refugee crises. However, on a per capita basis we are ranked well below most developed nations, with Sweden and other European countries contributing far more per capita. Furthermore, it is a sobering fact that, as a country, our actions have contributed directly or indirectly to some refugee crises. The Vietnam War—in Vietnam it is known as the American War—generated millions of refugees and displaced millions more. The Iraq War and the war in Afghanistan—wars in which our military played the dominant role—have also generated millions of refugees. Conversely, we have sometimes decided not to intervene in situations where there is little doubt that limited military action would have saved lives and reduced the number of refugees. Examples include our failure to intervene in the genocide in Rwanda and our delayed intervention in the Bosnian War. In every situation there are reasons for acting, or not acting, for intervening militarily or not, but the takeaway is that the welcoming of refugees to our country should not be based on abstract humanitarian grounds alone.

What emerged again and again, in the course of interviewing refugees for this book, was the enduring longing for one's country of birth, the profound validity of other ways of life. Thus many refugees, while having successfully adapted to life here, having found safety and their basic needs taken care of, continue to cherish the memory of their old lives. John Bul Dau, one of the Lost Boys of Sudan, makes a passionate case for this in his book *God Grew Tired of Us*:

> It was an ideal childhood. I would not trade our homeland for any other place on Earth. It is the land of our ancestors, the land of our cattle and our vegetables, the land we pass on to our descendants. I never questioned that I would live forever in this Eden.

Eden? He is talking about a place with unbearable numbers of mosquitoes, extreme heat and annual life-threatening food shortages, but for him and his brethren, home it was, and "home" it will always be.

After establishing themselves in the U.S. and becoming citizens, many refugees are able to visit their former homes. A number of Lost Boys of Sudan, after having lived here for many years, have returned to their now independent country (2011), South Sudan. Some have made the move permanent, and a few have even become members of parliament. On the other hand, many former refugees are prevented from returning to their country of birth, even for a visit. Still others have never even been to their ancestral homeland, as in the case of Tibetans whose parents fled Tibet, but who were themselves born in India. Tenzin Waser, whose parents were refugees, expresses this:

> I want to travel to Tibet. That's my most important place, but it's scary of course. This is our country but we are not comfortable with our country. We know our languages, but we are strangers in our own land.

In general, when refugees first arrive here, they are amazed by the personal freedom we Americans enjoy, by the physical safety most of us take for granted and by how well off we are. And while most new arrivals have almost no money, no possessions and no place of their own, their future

Joerg Boethling

Boys enjoying the fresh water of the Nile after the annual rains, South Sudan.

is full of hope. Upon arrival in America, refugees receive modest, short-term financial assistance to help get them on their feet. But for many, fully assimilating—or even regaining comparable status, professionally, socially and economically—remains an elusive goal, a goal typically not achieved by first-generation Americans. Consider the following all-too-typical scenario:

Suppose you are in your thirties or forties, have a college degree and have a good job teaching in your local high school. You speak three languages, including French. Your family is healthy and happy and you are a respected member of your community. But one day your house is destroyed, relatives are murdered, you and your family are forced to flee—from the place you have lived your entire life—and after ten or twenty years in refugee camps, you end up here. You need a job to support your family, but your credentials, when translated into English, are deemed inadequate. You are not qualified to teach in Vermont, nor anywhere else in the U.S. To be certified to teach you need to go back to college, but none of your three languages is spoken here. You need to take classes in English, but you need a job immediately. You take a low-paying job as a janitor, and thanks to your wages, together with your wife's income, you are able to provide for your family. Years pass; your children thrive, learn English perfectly and do well in school. It is they, not you, who are able to realize the American Dream.

4

Naturally, there are exceptions to this scenario. Val Kagan was the head of a large university research institute in his home city of Novosibirsk, Siberia, when increasing anti-Semitism during Perestroika (1991) forced him to leave Russia. With two PhDs and over 50 patents in his name, but speaking no English, his first job in Burlington was playing piano in a local restaurant. His potential was eventually realized, and Val went on to become chief scientist at the Hazelett Corporation in Colchester. Peter Deng, from South Sudan, has re-made himself twice. An orphan, he ran away from abusive relatives at age seven and grew up in refugee camps. A stellar student, he had almost completed college in Kenya when he was granted a visa to emigrate to the U.S. After a few years here, working as a janitor, he realized he was in a dead-end job and made the decision to get by on a part-time job in order to attend college. Today Peter is a CPA and has an MBA from Plymouth State University. He is a tax preparer in Burlington, and every year after tax season, he pays an extended visit to South Sudan to check on the businesses he has started there.

Worldwide, there are millions of people whose daily struggles—though not directly life-threatening—are so difficult or so limiting that leaving home, leaving one's country, is a compelling option. Ethnic and religious discrimination, food insecurity, family reunification, dismal job prospects and better education options are among the reasons that may drive immigration.

Modou Ndione

Modou Ndione teaching English in Dakar, Senegal.

Is assimilation a worthy goal or the loss of one's culture and identity? In the refugee or immigrant context, cultural assimilation is the process by which a person's language competency and cultural practices increasingly align with those of their adopted culture. Assimilation is considered complete when the degree of the immigrant's language fluency and observance of local traditions are indistinguishable from those of non-immigrants. While complete assimilation is rarely achieved by first-generation immigrants, it often is by the second generation, at least on the surface. Various factors affect the rate of assimilation, such as the size and cohesiveness of one's immigrant community and the degree to which religious practices and cultural attitudes differ between the two cultures, i.e. the cultural gap. Whether complete assimilation is a worthy goal is disputed. Clearly a degree of assimilation is desirable to function in the new environment, but the abandonment of traditional beliefs, customs and holidays—and especially the food one grew up with—can be likened to loss of one's self.

Our country has a long tradition of accepting refugees and immigrants. The Irish fleeing the Potato Famine, Italians seeking a better life, Scandinavians who settled in Wisconsin and Minnesota, Mexicans working the fields of

REUTERS/Mussa Qawasma

Palestinian woman, humiliated and threatened at an Israeli Army checkpoint near Hebron, West Bank, Israel, 2016.

REUTERS/Chris Helgren

During the months-long siege of Sarajevo, residents going about their daily errands crouch down to avoid Serb sniper fire, 1993.

California and more recent arrivals from Iraq, Bosnia, Somalia and Congo—all have made our relatively young country a country of immigrants. As President John Kennedy pointed out in his 1958 book *A Nation of Immigrants*,

> Another way of indicating the importance of immigration to America is to point out that every American who ever lived, with the exception of one group [Native Americans], was either an immigrant himself or a descendant of immigrants.

In recent years the greater Burlington area, and other locations in New England and throughout the United States, have seen an influx of refugees and immigrants. They have come for a variety of reasons and from many countries. Families and individuals from Bhutan, Somalia, Vietnam, Iraq, Myanmar, Tibet, Rwanda, Congo, Senegal and Bosnia have settled in our midst, and schools in Winooski and Burlington report as many as 30 languages spoken among their students.

These newcomers, refugees and immigrants alike, come from many different backgrounds, and their cultural traditions and individual histories present a unique opportunity for us "natives" to learn about the world outside the United States. Perhaps their most noticeable impact is the profusion of such restaurants, as Pho Hong in Burlington's Old North End, Sherpa Kitchen and Hong's Dumplings in Burlington, Tiny Thai in Winooski and many others. Ethnic grocery stores are popping up: Iraqi-owned Nada Market in Winooski, Bhutanese-owned Central Market, Euro Market (Bosnian) and Winooski's Spicy Land Asian Supermarket (Vietnamese-American), to name just a few.

There are many organizations worldwide, large and small, assisting refugees by supplying food, providing shelter and medical help and assisting with resettlement and repatriation. Worldwide, the primary relief organization is UNHCR, the UN's Refugee Agency. Other organizations include Save the Children, International Refugee Committee, Catholic Charities USA, Office of Refugee Resettlement and Doctors Without Borders.

The primary organizations working with refugees in Vermont are VRRP (Vermont Refugee and Resettlement Program) and AALV (Association of Africans living in Vermont).

Norwegian Refugee Council

The Norwegian Refugee Council, an independent humanitarian organization, provided assistance to over nine million refugees and displaced persons in 2017. Above, NRC's media director on a visit to South Sudan.

Vermont's refugee resettlement organization is a field office of the U.S. Committee for Refugees and Immigrants (USCRI). Based in Colchester and known up until recently as the Vermont Refugee Resettlement Program, or VRRP, its title is now USCRI Vermont. The program, directed by Amila Merdzanovic, herself a refugee from Bosnia, helps refugee families and individuals from the moment they arrive and provides ongoing assistance as they adapt to life in this country. USCRI Vermont focuses on giving refugees the tools to start their new lives in Vermont by providing client-centered services, including case management to help with all aspects of transition to the life in the U.S., employment assistance focused on achieving self-sufficiency, medical case management to ensure that health needs are addressed, English language classes, interpretation and translation services, family strengthening workshops and community engagement. Additionally, a robust local network of volunteers and community partners provides essential support to USCRI Vermont through tutoring, mentoring, transportation, apartment setup and administrative help.

The Association of Africans living in Vermont (AALV), though originally created to assist Burlington's small African community, decided in 2009 to offer its services to all refugee groups in Vermont, and by 2018, AALV was able to provide legal services to 694 individuals from 67 countries. Refugees from Bhutan, Somalia, the Democratic Republic of Congo, Republic of Congo, Iraq and Nepal made up about 75% of the cases. Through workforce development, health awareness, interpreter services and various classes and courses, AALV plays a crucial, ongoing role in helping New Americans from all parts of the world—regardless of race, ethnic group, religion, political affiliation or sexual orientation—make a successful transition to life here in Vermont.

The experiences of New Americans in our midst provide us with insight into the challenges of adapting to an alien culture, our own American culture. This in turn shines a light on our traditions and beliefs. The goal of this book is to show, by relating the life stories of individuals who have experienced profound loss and extreme hardship, that starting over in a foreign land, through determination and hard work, it is possible to achieve a measure of success and happiness. This achievement deserves our acceptance and respect. This collection of stories from all over the world, together with related historical backgrounds, will go some way toward informing and expanding the worldview of its readers.

BHUTAN

Bhutan is a small Asian country bordering India and Tibet (China). Most westerners who have knowledge of the country know it as an exotic travel destination. Indeed, it is a sparsely populated land of incredible scenery, with the Himalayan range forming its northern border. Bhutan is also known, and admired for, its remarkable preservation of many aspects of its traditional culture. Beautiful, elaborate Tibetan-style monasteries in fantastic settings, a king and queen in their royal palace, the local populace dressed in colorful traditional attire and a deliberate, measured approach to outside influences help bolster Bhutan's image as a land that is managing the transition from a closed medieval kingdom to a modern society while preserving its unique Buddhist culture.

Bhutan's cultural uniformity, as promoted by the Tourism Council of Bhutan and admired by Western tourists, is not without its detractors. It's no surprise that not every Bhutanese is thrilled to wear only the approved national costume, to have his or her hair cut in the standard fashion and to confirm to various other edicts. However, objections of this nature are insignificant compared to those raised by Bhutanese who are of Nepalese origin, the Lhotshampas.

Starting as early as the 17th century, Nepalis were invited to immigrate to Bhutan. Valued for their artisan skills and to help develop the country's agriculture, they settled in the uninhabited southern part of the country. Over time, the Lhotshampas' hard work paid off, as jungle areas were converted to prosperous farming communities, and the south became an essential source of the county's food supply. As they grew better educated, the Lhotshampas began to question their status as second-class citizens in their own country and agitated for better access to jobs, more personal freedom and a more representative role in government.

However, by the 1980s, King Jigme Singey Wangchuck, the fourth king of Bhutan, had grown increasingly concerned about the country's large, and fast-growing, ethnic Nepalese population. The predominantly Hindu and culturally distinct Nepalese were seen to be in conflict with—and a threat to—the Tibetan-style Buddhist image that Bhutan sought to promote and preserve. The official motto now, as then, is "One country, one people." The results of the country's first census, in 1988, shocked the ruling elite,

The sacred Tiger's Nest monastery of Bhutan, built in 1692.

as it showed the Lhotshampas were almost as numerous as the favored northern population, the Drukpa people. (Drukpas migrated into the area now known as Bhutan from Tibet in the ninth century.)

The fear was that the rapidly growing Nepali-speaking southerners might soon outnumber the ruling Drukpa. To combat this, a complex, arbitrarily administered definition of citizenship was immediately implemented. The result was that many thousands of Lhotsampas found themselves no longer considered citizens of Bhutan. Many had their citizenship documents confiscated. This was the background for the subsequent expulsion of over 100,000 Lhotshampas from Bhutan in the 1990s. It is important to note that the individuals being forced out of Bhutan were born and raised in Bhutan. People whose parents (and, in many cases, grandparents) were born and raised in Bhutan, were being expelled from the only country they had ever known. Although there is no exact parallel in this country, the cruelty of Bhutan's actions can be compared to the U.S. deciding to deport all individuals of, say, Italian descent, except that in the case of Bhutan, we are talking about a much larger percentage of the population, almost 20%.

Typical Lhotshampa home, southern Bhutan.

Morning prayers at the start of the school day, refugee camp in Jhapa, Nepal.

To summarize the chain of events that led to the expulsion of Lhotshampas, in 1989 and 1990, as their protests against the government—at times violent—spread throughout the country, the king responded by moving army units south into Lhotshampa territory. Schools and religious seminaries were abruptly closed, businesses shuttered, property confiscated and a policy of general harassment initiated. Intimidated and terrified by the torture, imprisonment, rape and executions perpetrated by the soldiers, many began to flee to nearby India. For those who refused to leave, harassment continued unabated. People were given a choice: give up your Nepali language, your Hindu religion, your cultural traditions and follow the official edicts and you will be allowed to stay. Otherwise, leave the country. Many who hesitated were forced at gunpoint to sign documents attesting to their "voluntary decision" to leave. Entire families left on very short notice (often only 24 hours) forfeiting their homes and businesses, their farms and their livestock—everything but a few meager possessions. Most passed quickly through India, continuing directly to provisional refugee camps in southeastern Nepal (to the area known as Jhapa), only a three- to five-hour drive from the border of Bhutan—that is, about as far as from Burlington, Vermont, to Boston.

Years passed, and gradually the international community, including the UN, responded to the plight of the Lhotshampas. The refugee camps were initially rife with malnutrition and measles, TB, malaria and scurvy, although camp conditions improved markedly after 1995. The schooling provided to the refugees in the Nepalese camps was relatively good, but the camps remained significantly overcrowded through 2006. While some refugees have been able to integrate into Nepalese society, officially Nepal does not allow this, and the Bhutanese government is steadfast in its refusal to repatriate its former citizens. At present (2018), most of the refugees have been resettled out of the camps to countries all over the world. The majority, about 100,000, have been resettled in the U.S. Incredibly, most refugees languished in the camps for over 20 years, and during this time thousands of children were born. Since the education system in Nepal (and India) is a legacy of the British era, even minimally educated individuals arrive here with a basic grasp of English. This English proficiency has been a major factor in the Bhutanese community's successful transition to life in this country.

Rice terraces, southern Bhutan.

Refugee camp fire in 2008 that destroyed over 1,000 huts, leaving 8,000 people without shelter, Jhapa, Nepal.

In summary, Bhutan, as a Buddhist-based monarchy, has apparently succeeded in its efforts to eliminate the perceived threat posed by its Nepali-speaking Hindu minority. Bhutan is the originator and promoter of the Gross National Happiness metric, and it claims that its people are among the happiest in the world. Yet, ironically, Bhutan continues to deny its history of persecution and expulsion of about 20% of its citizens.

Many exiled Bhutanese have friends and relatives still living in Bhutan, and only now, after almost 30 years, are some of these individuals able to obtain Bhutanese citizenship. But for those who were forced out of Bhutan, returning to their former homes in Bhutan, even as visitors, is not permitted by the authorities.

‖‖‖

Bidur Dahal

BHUTAN

Bidur comes from a prominent and successful family. His father was an important Hindu priest, one uncle was a member of Bhutan's Parliament and another was a customs official. His parents placed a strong emphasis on education and were not politically active. Bidur, his parents and seven siblings owned a productive farm in the warm southern part of the country—his family had sufficient rice and other food supplies on hand to last them two years. The cardamom trees in their garden provided the family with an ample supply of the treasured spice—essential to Nepalese cooking—and a valuble cash crop. In short, theirs was a happy, prosperous existence. Today his family is scattered all over the world, but none of them lives in Bhutan.

In 1989, when Bidur was 14, relations between the culturally distinct northern and southern regions of Bhutan had deteriorated to the point of violence. Threatened by the prosperity of the fast-growing, hard-working and well-educated Hindu population in the south of the country, the northerners—the king and the ruling Ngalop ethnic group—devised and promoted a policy known as One Country, One People. Implementation of this policy meant that Bhutan's ethnic Nepalis—known as Lhotsampas— had to abandon much of their culture: convert to the Buddhist faith, use a language different from their native Nepali and even conform to the country's national dress code. Rejection of these unreasonable demands, coupled with an increased desire on the part of the Lhotsampas for a greater say in the government, soon led to violent protests. As a response to this, in 1990 the military took over control of the south, and normal life for Bidur and his family—and many thousands of others—came to an abrupt end. Schools were converted into military barracks, property was confiscated and people were threatened and beaten.

Bizarre requirements regarding citizenship were announced, making many thousands effectively stateless. Everyone was given a choice: convert to the accepted way of life or leave the country. Resistance—or even a minor delay in complying with orders—was met with arrest. Murders were committed, and soldiers raped local women with impunity. Bidur relates that in many instances, the military demanded that villages turn over some of their young women to the soldiers. People were forced from their homes with days' or only hours' notice. "Voluntary" relinquishment of citizenship and property at gunpoint was common. Ultimately one-sixth of the country's population was forced out of Bhutan.

Because Bidur's father is a high priest, his family was spared for a time, but gradually even he came under increasing pressure to "convert." When he refused, their family home was harassed night after night with searchlights, making sleep impossible. On a tip that he was about to be arrested, Bidur's father, together with Bidur's mother and other family members fled to India. The rest of the family left a few days later, taking the barest of possessions with them. In the pouring rain—it was monsoon season—they left home in the middle of the night and fled on foot through the jungle and across the border to India. Since the fleeing Bhutanese were ethnic Nepalis, India felt able to justify escorting them directly onward to nearby Nepal, although most of them had never set foot in Nepal and had nowhere to go once there. But Nepal took them in, and there they languished, grouped together in primitive refugee camps, on average for about twenty years!

Initially life in the camps was terrible, and many died from disease and starvation. Gradually conditions improved, especially after the UN and other relief agencies realized what had transpired in Bhutan. Strangely, the fact that Bhutan expelled over 100,000 of its law-abiding citizens is not well known, even today. Known in the West primarily as an exotic travel destination, Bhutan has succeeded in preserving the dominance of its ancestral

Home sweet home in the refugee camp. Bidur lower right.

Tibetan-Buddhist traditions and presents itself as having a wholesome way of life, rooted in ancient traditions, while entering the modern world in a measured and deliberate fashion, with happiness for all.

A top student, Bidur was able to finish high school while living in the camp. Based on his placement in the regional exams—he came in second out of thousands of students—he won a scholarship to a university in Kathmandu. In Kathmandu he lived alone in a tiny apartment, and since his scholarship paid only his school expenses, it was a struggle to make ends meet, forcing him to go without food at times. But he stayed the course and graduated after four years. In the following years he worked at various jobs in Nepal and India as a reporter, editor, researcher, teacher and administrator.

When he decided to apply to graduate school, Bidur's excellent university record gained him a full scholarship to the Asian Institute of Technology in Bangkok, Thailand. During the next two years, young, unattached

Bidur found himself in a stimulating university environment, in an exciting city and with no money worries. According to Bidur, *These were the golden years of my life.*

He completed a master's degree in Environmental Technology and Management and returned to his refugee camp to apply for a visa to the U.S. While waiting for his visa to come through—it took three years—he married "the girl next door" and taught school to support himself and his wife. Finally, in 2009, he and Radika were able to immigrate to the United States, where in 2010 their son was born.

Katie Figura

Krish, Radika, Siya and Bidur on a cold January day.

His first job here was as a sales associate. But following stints as a translator, a teacher's aide and a medical case manager for VRRP, Vermont's Refugee Resettlement Program, he is now employed with the University of Vermont College of Medicine as an Education Coach–Outreach Professional in the Vermont LEND Program (Leadership Education in Developmental Disabilities). He is founding director, a board member and secretary of the Vermont Hindu Temple, which is located in Burlington. Until recently, Radika worked as a Licensed Nurse's Aid (LNA) but has recently transitioned to a new career as a Vermont board-certified cosmetologist. In summary, both Bidur and his wife have made a successful transition to life here.

While they are happy with where they live, they look forward to a future, where as Bidur puts it:

> I would like to own my own home, have a career in the education field, have my kids succeed so that they will be able to support themselves and, later in life, support us.

As far as paying a visit to Bhutan, it is still not possible for Bidur to visit the country of his birth. He is not allowed into the country even on a normal U.S. tourist visa. Bhutan is unique in that tourism is tightly controlled—tourists are usually allowed in only as part of an approved group with a pre-approved itinerary and with a certified local guide. It is also expensive, as the government requires each visitor to pay a fee of 250 dollars per day. Thus, the freedom of movement and flexible itineraries that travelers enjoy in neighboring countries—Nepal, India, Thailand, for example—are not an option in Bhutan's case.

||||

Deoki Gurung

BHUTAN

Deoki was born into a farming family in the Himalayan kingdom
of Bhutan. About 50 percent larger than Vermont, Bhutan has
a population about the size of Vermont's. The country is famous for its
beautiful mountain landscapes and Tibetan-style Buddhist culture. Its
exotic, fairytale quality, combined with a well-managed tourist industry,
have made it a coveted destination for adventurous travelers.

Deoki's family has lived in Bhutan for several generations but was
originally from Nepal, her great-grandfather having settled in Bhutan at
a time when Nepali craftsmen were encouraged to immigrate to Bhutan.
She is an ethnic Nepali, and, as her last name indicates, her family belongs
to the Gurung caste, one of the many subgroups in Nepal. However, like
thousands of ethnic Nepalis from Bhutan—over 100,000 in fact—she has
neither Bhutanese nor Nepalese citizenship and is essentially unwelcome in
both countries. Her background is typical of most of the adult Bhutanese
now living in Vermont and elsewhere in the U.S.

Deoki's mother died when Deoki was four, and when she was five,
her father left, leaving her in the care of his brother's family. Deoki has
a younger sister, and when their father left, he took her sister with him
and subsequently either sold or gave her away. When Deoki was six, in

Beldangi-2, the refugee camp in southern Nepal where Deoki spent 18 years and where her two older children were born.

1992, the expulsion of ethnic Nepalis from Bhutan was underway, and she and most of her relatives fled to neighboring Nepal. The local authorities had given them 24 hours to leave the country, threatening to destroy their houses or kill them if they didn't comply. Nepal refused them normal status and placed them in makeshift refugee camps. Thousands still live in these camps, 27 years later. Deoki grew up in the huge Beldangi Refugee Camp in southeastern Nepal. In all, she spent 18 years there.

Fortunately, her camp was located in the warm lowlands of southeastern Nepal (the area known as Jhapa), and staying warm was relatively easy, but in the early years, malaria and other tropical diseases posed a serious problem. The standard camp dwelling was a bamboo hut with a thatched roof made from bamboo strips. Water for cooking and drinking was available from a communal spigot for two hours in the morning and two hours in the evening. Overcrowding and abysmal sanitation aggravated an already grim existence. On a positive note, children in the camps received relatively good schooling.

When Deoki was 15, she married. To clarify, her grandfather arranged her marriage to the son of a friend of his, someone she had never met. Her husband was 17. Deoki, as is the custom, moved into the home of her in-laws, who lived in a different section of the camp, essentially cutting off contact with the loving, supportive grandmother who had taken care of her since she was eight. In Deoki's words: *Grand Mom really loved me a lot.* For Deoki, a young bride living with her husband's family, further schooling was out of the question. And, as is typical, Deoki had low status in her husband's family and could look forward to many years of thankless toil: scouring the nearby hills for firewood, carrying it back to camp, cooking, cleaning and doing other chores assigned to her.

When Deoki was 16 her daughter Meera was born, followed two years later by a son, Saliesh. As is typical in many impoverished areas of Nepal, most men in the camp must leave the area to find work. Thus her husband was gone for six to eight months at a time, and with no help in raising her kids, Deoki's already tough existence became even more grim.

Finally, when she was 24, she was able to leave for the U.S. with official refugee status, and she, her husband and their two kids left the refugee camp existence behind. They relocated to Winooski and moved in with her in-laws, who had immigrated to Vermont the year before.

Moving to the U.S. has made a huge difference for Deoki. What does she think of America? *It is better, better than Nepal. I am free.* An accomplished seamstress, her first job was at Vermont Teddy Bear in Shelburne. As an indication of how long full participation in "our" world can take, during her first four years here, Deoki never visited Burlington's Church Street. In fact, she never set foot in Burlington, except to change buses. But this was not for lack of interest; with no car, no one to show her around and very little free time, her world was no larger than absolutely necessary. After two years at Vermont Teddy Bear, Deoki was hired as the cook at the popular Namasté Restaurant in Winooski—a job she loved—and worked six days a week, 12 to 14 hours a day. She soon got her driver's license and was able to buy her first car, a white Jeep Cherokee.

In 2015, owner Tonny Thanh sold Namasté Restaurant and established Pho Thao Restaurant and Grocery on North Avenue in Burlington's New

North End, taking Deoki, now divorced, with him. Only two years later, in late 2017, Tonny bought back Namasté Restaurant, naming it Dharsan Namasté Asian Deli. In May 2018, he opened a grocery store less than a block up Main Street from Namasté Asian Deli.

Deoki, now 33, is a stay-home mother. The two of them—Deoki, Bhutanese, and Tonny, Vietnamese-American—are in a committed relationship and have a baby daughter. Deoki doesn't speak Vietnamese and Tonny doesn't speak Nepali, so their common language is English.

At some point, when she's saved enough money, Deoki would like to take a trip back to Nepal to visit relatives and friends still living in the refugee camps. However, travel to Bhutan is not an option for her—at least not to the area where she was born—nor does it have much appeal: she has no memories of Bhutan, and almost none of her relatives still live there.

Born in Hue, Vietnam, to an American soldier and a Vietnamese mother, Tonny was born after the Army had transferred his father back to the States. Once the war ended, out of fear of reprisal—possibly death—at the hands of the Viet Cong, Tonny's mother destroyed all evidence of her relationship with Tonny's father, including his Social Security card and other documents—documents that she was to have used to find him in the

Jared Gange

Deoki (right of center), with her two of her kids and her best friend Muna in 2015.

Matt Thorsen for *Seven Days*

Tonny applying real heat to the stir fry.

States after the war. But this did not prevent beatings at the hands of the Viet Cong. Tonny still bears scars on his legs, and he was never allowed to attend school. Tonny would give almost anything to find his dad, but with almost nothing to go on, his efforts to date have been unsuccessful.

RITA NEOPANEY

BHUTAN

Rita grew up in a well-to-do family in the south of Bhutan. Her grandfather was a successful businessman, and by the time Rita came along, her father was running the family grocery store, her two uncles ran their clothing store and her grandfather was managing the restaurant. Their farms supplied cardamom and oranges to nearby markets in India. With several successful enterprises, employing a number of people, this was a prosperous existence by any measure. But in 1990, through no fault of theirs, this existence began to unravel.

Following implementation of Bhutan's Citizenship Act of 1985, which redefined and severely restricted the definition of Bhutanese citizenship, Bhutan's large Nepali population—known as Lhotshampas—was forced to conform to an officially defined lifestyle, or leave the country. Converting to the approved lifestyle meant abandoning their religion and transitioning to speaking Dzongkha—the language of the dominant Ngalop population—instead of their native Nepali. The vast majority of Lhotshampas were unwilling or unable to do so. As a consequence, thousands of Bhutanese citizens, despite having been born and raised in Bhutan—and having lived their entire lives in Bhutan—were categorized as illegal aliens. Starting in 1991, when the Bhutanese army occupied the southern region of the country, home to most of the Lhotshampas, many thousands—ultimately over 100,000—were forced from their homes and out of the country. For the most part they fled through neighboring India to Nepal, their ancestral homeland. This was the plight of Rita and her extended family.

When government representatives asked Rita's grandfather—the head of the family—what his plans for the future were under the new law, his response was that he planned to continue life as before. This did not sit well with the authorities, and, based on a tip that the army was moving to arrest him, he and the other male members of Rita's family promptly left for Nepal.

After the men left the country, Rita's mother and grandmother did their best to manage the businesses, but after four months, enduring constant harassment and living in an environment of widespread abuse by the police and government soldiers—imprisonment, beatings and rape—they gathered their kids and a few basic possessions and fled to Nepal as well. In doing so, they forfeited their homes and property. They never received compensation from the Bhutanese government, a government that only recently, and to only a very limited degree, has taken responsibility for its treatment of the ethnic Nepalis living in Bhutan.

Traveling by truck through India to Nepal, Rita and her family members reached Maidhar, a hastily constructed refugee camp in southeastern Nepal. At that time, in 1992, conditions at Maidhar were unspeakably bad with overcrowding, poor sanitation facilities, and rampant disease. Rita estimates that every day 30–40 bodies had to be disposed of. She lived in this cesspool of a place for a year and a half. Gradually the United Nations Refugee Agency and other relief organizations responded to their plight and built camps to a somewhat higher standard. But even in the newer camps, conditions were horrible, according to Rita. The food rations were barely enough to survive on, and residents were dependent on donations for clothes. By the time she moved to the new Beldangi-2 camp, Rita was 13 years old. In all, Rita lived 18 years in refugee camps. Fortunately, schooling was available inside the confines of the camp, and Rita completed the tenth grade there.

She attended grades 11 and 12 at a private school in the nearby city of Biratnagar. She then taught math and social studies for a year, making enough money to pay for her younger sister's education, before going on to college. In college, her daily routine was to take classes in the morning, teach in the afternoon and receive tutoring from her professors in the evening. After her second year of college, Rita married Khara, a fellow Bhutanese. Khara was paid enough as a teacher to support the two of them, making it possible for her to concentrate full-time on her studies. After she received her degree, Rita joined Khara in Kathmandu, where he was teaching, and got a job as school coordinator for staff of 12 teachers. In 2008, after eight years in Kathmandu, she, Khara and their son were given the green light to immigrate to America—to New York City—as Bhutanese refugees.

After two years in New York, Rita and Khara moved to Burlington, where their second child, Rewaj, was born. While life in New York was interesting and exciting, the couple felt Vermont would be a better place to raise a family. Initially Rita got a job working part-time as a Nepali translator for the Association of Africans Living in Vermont (AALV), a support organization for recently arrived refugees. She now works there full-time as a caseworker and counselor. She also teaches classes in parenting skills and family finances and is AALV's Community Outreach Counselor and Program Specialist, specializing in community and domestic violence

Katie Figura

Rita with her husband Khara and sons Rejos and Rewaj.

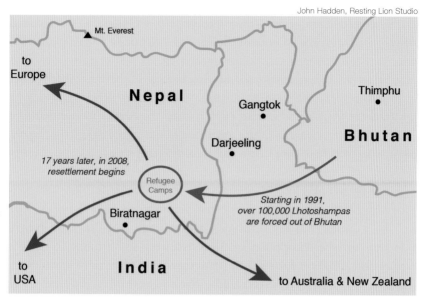

John Hadden, Resting Lion Studio

The expulsion of Bhutanese of Nepali origin from their homes in Bhutan to refugee camps in Nepal and their subsequent resettlement in other countries 17 years later.

education and counseling. Thus Rita plays a key role in helping newcomers from different traditions and backgrounds adapt to our American way of life. She speaks three languages besides English—Nepali, Hindi and Dzongkha. As she puts it: *Life is way more better here. It's easy if you understand the rules and regulations in this country.*

Rita's husband, although well educated with a master's degree in mathematics education, has had a harder time finding satisfactory employment here. For example, it took him seven years to find meaningful, reasonably well paid work: when they lived in New York City, he worked as a dishwasher. His poor English skills were part of the problem, but as Rita describes his initial years here:

> Since my husband is from a minority culture, and due [to] the cultural silence of his person, his voice was unheard and unrecognized. As such, relevant employment based on his education and experience was denied him.

Today Khara is employed as a case manager with Age Well, an organization dedicated to providing aging Vermonters with the assistance necessary to keep them healthy and independent.

His case exemplifies the plight of many immigrants who come here as adults with established careers in their home countries. It is very difficult, even with good language skills, to make a lateral career move from one's home country to a new country because the differing languages, education systems, job requirements and credentials present formidable barriers to a smooth transition.

Most of Rita's family has now settled here in the U.S., but making the adjustment to life in a different country is an ongoing process, especially for older family members. Thus, not unlike many older Vermonters, her mother, father and grandfather (93), after enduring Vermont's cold winters for years, recently moved south to a warmer climate.

Rita and Khara own their house in Burlington's New North End, where they live with their two sons, now aged fifteen and eight. Everyone in the family is a U.S citizen and the boys do well in school. She does worry about her sons losing touch with their culture: *I am scared in one part of my brain that my kids will forget their culture and forget the Nepali language.* Rejos, her older son, is a promising football player and is applying to schools out of state, hoping to play on a Division I team—not a possibility in Vermont—his last two years of high school.

While she has relatives still living in Bhutan, she has no immediate plans to visit. Visiting Bhutan, while theoretically possible, now that Rita is an American citizen, has little appeal, as she would almost certainly not be allowed to visit relatives still living in the part of Bhutan where she spent her early life. Bhutan is also expensive for tourists; all non-official visitors are required to pay $250 per day. As far as Rita knows, no one from Burlington's 3,000-strong Bhutanese community has paid a return visit to the country that was once home.

BOSNIA-HERZEGOVINA

The southeastern European region just across the Adriatic Sea from Italy was known until 1995 as Yugoslavia. Popular with European vacationers summer and winter for its food, culture and recreation opportunities, it is a mountainous region featuring fantastic beaches and ancient cities along its Mediterranean coast. The Bosnian city of Sarajevo, the second largest in the region, was the site of the 1984 Winter Olympics. With the Adriatic Sea on the west, Austria and Hungary to the north, Bulgaria and Romania to the east and Greece and Albania on its southern border, this area has for centuries been a complex, interrelated mix of languages, cultures and religious traditions. The area was, and is today, made up of a number of sub-states: Croatia, Serbia and Bosnia-Herzegovina, among others. Three ethnic groups, defined along religious lines, make up most of the population. *Croats* are primarily Catholic and *Serbs* are overwhelmingly Eastern Orthodox Christian. *Bosnians* are more mixed. Their largest, and dominant, group is Muslim, but significant percentages of Serbs and Croats identify as Bosnian.

In April 1991, Serbia attacked neighboring Croatia, and soon the region was embroiled in a horrific conflict that ultimately consumed most of Yugoslavia. The ensuing fighting and atrocities—known as the Bosnian War—were of such barbarity that they defy comprehension. The country was torn apart, neighbor was pitted against neighbor, coworker against coworker. Sarajevo, a city of almost half a million people and the capital of the Muslim-majority Bosnian republic, was encircled and blockaded by Serbian forces. For almost four years, Serb fighters terrorized the citizens of Sarajevo with artillery and sniper fire from the surrounding hills. The war saw 130,000 to 140,000 killed and generated about two million refugees and internally displaced persons. After the war, the former Yugoslavia split into five independent countries, Bosnia-Herzegovina, Serbia, Croatia, Slovenia and Macedonia, and later, in 2006, Montenegro achieved nation status.

What was the cause of this war?

To attempt to answer this question, it is helpful to look back to World War II. During that war, control of Yugoslavia was bitterly contested by the Allies (British) and the Axis Powers (Germany and Italy). Yugoslavs fought

Sunset over Sarajevo, Bosnia and Herzegovina's capital.

on one side or the other, or against both. Josep Broz, "Tito," a particularly effective and charismatic partisan fighter, emerged as Yugoslavia's leader after the war. Tito managed to hold the country's diverse regions and ethnic groups together as one country until his death in 1980. Known as the "benevolent dictator" and nominally communist, Tito successfully steered the "Socialist Federal Republic of Yugoslavia" on a path independent of the Soviet Union. But after his death, followed by the disintegration of the Soviet Union in 1991 and subsequent hard economic times, conditions were ripe for the region's underlying ethnic grievances to assert themselves.

In 1991, Serbia (Bosnia's neighbor to the east), under the leadership of President Slobodan Milosevic, undertook a campaign of aggressively advancing Serbian nationalism, with the ultimate goal of creating a larger Serbian state incorporating *any and all* territory with significant Serbian population. An essential component of the Serbian effort was the use of television and radio to spread a message of ethnic rivalry and distrust. By promoting ethnic hatred and reviving ancient disputes, the relatively harmonious coexistence that had been the norm shattered was shattered by this campaign. In short order Serbs, Croats and Muslims—who had lived peacefully together for their entire lives, accepting each other's ethnic backgrounds—began to regard each other as enemies. Serbs, both from Serbia itself and from within Bosnia, initiated the conflict by attacking Croatia, and then Bosnia, as these republics asserted their right to independence.

Characterized by brutal torture, senseless destruction of cities and homes and the mass slaughter of non-combatants, the Bosnian War produced war crimes not seen in Europe since World War II. The 1995 genocide in the Bosnia-Herzegovinian city of Srebrenica—the cold-blooded execution of over 8,000 Muslim civilians—is considered the worst atrocity in Europe since the Holocaust. Although Croats and Bosnians carried out atrocities against Serbs, and each other, the conflict is overwhelmingly characterized by the persecution of Bosnian Muslims by the Serbs. The war was ultimately stopped by a NATO bombing campaign—initiated by the United States— directed at Serb military positions, and by American-led negotiations that culminated in the Dayton Peace Accords.

Mark Milstein, Dreamstime

A Serb tank rolls through the countryside, 1992.

Annual burial ceremony for victims of the Srebrenica Genocide, forensically identified during the previous year. The number of civilians murdered is written on the mourner's shirt.

Trials of Serbian war criminals continue to this day. Serbian president Milosevic died in prison while on trial in the Hague, at the UN-established International Tribunal for the former Yugoslavia. Radovan Karadzic, the president of the Serb Republic within Bosnia, and the presumed architect of many actions against Muslims, particularly in Sarajevo and Srebrenica, has been sentenced to 40 years in prison. The trial of Ratko Mladic, the Serbian commander in charge of the atrocities in Srebrenica, culminated in a life sentence. He was convicted on 11 counts of crimes against humanity and violations of the customs of war, among them genocide, extermination, murder, deportation, attacks on civilians and the taking of hostages.

Before the war, Bosnia's multi-culturalism and religious tolerance gave credence to the possibility of a harmonious, multi-ethnic society. Today, over 20 years later, peace and political stability again prevail across the region, but Bosnian and Serb dissatisfaction with the terms of the Dayton Peace Accords inhibits a return to the previous level of peaceful coexistence. As part of the peace plan, the Bosnian side agreed to give up considerable land and several important cities to Serb control, thus allowing the creation of a Serbian sub-state, Republika Srpska (Republic of Serbia), within Bosnia. Thus, while Bosnia (Bosnia-Herzegovina) has retained its prewar international boundaries, it now consists of two territorries approximately equal in size, each with its own government—an arrangement considered by some to be the world's most complicated system of government. Bosnian Muslims and Croats govern what is referred to as the Federation of Bosnia and Herzegovina, and Bosnian Serbs control Srpska. The combined country is known as Bosnia-Herzegovina. This fact state of affairs represents

Dreamstime

Child's coffin, fashioned from the stadium seats used during Sarajevo's 1984 Winter Olympics.

a victory for the Serbian war aims: Indeed, the creation of Serb a "statelet" within Bosnia was a primary goal of Ratko Mladic, Radovan Karadzic and other Serbian nationalists. Thus, particularly for Bosnian Muslims, any sense that justice has been done by the prosecution of these Serbian leaders is almost completely nullified.

After the war, many displaced Bosnians found it impossible to return home, finding their houses destroyed or occupied by Serbs. Entire regions that had existed as ethnically mixed societies, were now under the control of a Serbian regime intent on erasing all traces of Muslim heritage. For instance, the rebuilding of mosques destroyed in the war is consistently obstructed. The intermingling of ethnic groups has accordingly diminished, as Muslims on the one hand, and Serbs on the other, increasingly concentrate in their respective territories. As Bosnia–Herzegovina works toward admission to the European Union, it is a worrisome fact that Serb nationalism is on the rise. The leading political figure in Sprska, Milorad Dodik, is an outspoken secessionist and is actively rebuilding his country's arsenal, an activity explicitly banned in the Dayton Peace Accords. The concern is that by attempting to annex neighboring territories, the Serbian expansionist goal of a Greater Serbia will re-ignite war in the region.

The peace that has been achieved is a frail and guarded peace. Nurturing it is an ongoing process, because the war was so brutal and the peace agreement so problematic. Sadly, rather than being characterized as peace, the status quo is often described as the absence of war.

Many thousands of Bosnian Muslims have received international refugee status, with the majority immigrating to the U.S. and Europe. This is the background shared by the over 2,000 Bosnians living in the Burlington area, most of whom are now U.S. citizens.

▌▌▌▌

ADNA KARABEGOVIC

BOSNIA

dna was born in Banja Luka, the second largest city in Bosnia. Set in the verdant Vrbas River Valley, Banja Luka is famous for its many fountains, kayaking, downtown pedestrian area and parks. Prior to the start of the Bosnian War, Banja Luka was regarded as a model of religious tolerance and multi-ethnic acceptance; its neighborhoods were diverse and a general love for the quality of life in Banja Luka was shared among its citizens. When the war broke out in the early 1990s, any semblance of peaceful coexistence quickly evaporated. In an atmosphere of increasing hostility from Serbs, both civilian and military, most of the Muslim and non-Serb population began to flee the city. As threats escalated in Banja Luka, Adna's mother, sister and Adna escaped from Banja Luka on one of the last buses out of town to Belgrade, in order to catch a plane to Berlin, Germany. That summer, Adna was turning three years old and her sister Dzeneta five. Soon thereafter, safe departure from Banja Luka was almost impossible for non-Serbs.

In Berlin, the three of them moved in with Adna's grandmother and step-grandfather in their one-bedroom apartment. Two months would pass before Adna's father was able to escape Bosnia and join his family. Those two months were spent in hiding, moving from house to house, avoiding the Serbian authorities, as able-bodied Muslim men were forced by the Serbs to

Dreamstime

The reconstructed historic Ferhadija mosque in Banja Luka, destroyed by Serbian forces during the Bosnian War.

either fight alongside them or work as slave laborers. The latter option involved assisting with the pilfering of Muslim homes that had been confiscated, and, in the worst cases, witnessing and cleaning up after attacks on fellow Muslims.

During the war, Banja Luka experienced a brutal program of ethnic cleansing, and Muslim families, like the Karabegovics, were prime targets. Constant harassment, robbery, beatings, rape, murder, confiscation of property, forced labor—all condoned by the Serbian authorities—were the order of the day. The city began to change as its cultural sites became prime targets during the aggression: all of Banja Luka's mosques were burned to the ground, as well as Catholic architectural and cultural objects, such as the Franciscan monastery in Petričevac. The Serbification of Banja Luka attempted to rid the city of the non-Serb population and eradicate any remnant of their history.

In Berlin, Adna and Dzeneta settled into their new existence: the family moved into a small apartment in one of the Turkish "ghettos" prior to moving to a more affluent area in Berlin. These were fun times for Adna as she could run wild and carefree in their neighborhood. She and her sister attended the German schools and naturally became fluent in German. As they adapted to life in Germany, the two of them began speaking German to one another so much that Adna's command of the Bosnian language began to fade.

Her father was fortunate to be able to pursue his occupation as an architect and her mother worked as a volunteer in schools set up for

Ramirez, WikiCommons

The Bosnian city of Mostar and its famed Islamic-style bridge, built in the 16th century by the Ottoman Turks. It was destroyed during the Bosnian War and rebuilt in 2004.

Bosnian refugees. All told, their lives in Berlin were satisfactory, but after six years, their temporary permission to stay in Germany was terminated. Peace had been achieved in Bosnia, and it was expected that they, along with other Bosnian refugees, would either return home to Bosnia, or take up permanent residence in another country. For Adna and her family, returning to Banja Luka was not an option, because, according to the terms of the American-brokered peace agreement that brought the war to a close (Dayton Peace Accords), with the subsequent redrawing of Bosnia's borders, their hometown was included in the newly defined Serb sub-state (Republika Srpska) within Bosnia-Herzegovina. Thus, for them, Banja Luka was both unwelcoming and not particularly safe, as it was now legitimately controlled by the enemy. Fortunately, to their surprise and relief, about this time they received word that they were cleared to immigrate to the U.S. With less than a month's notice, they hurriedly packed, and, leaving their lives in Germany behind, arrived in Burlington in May of 1998. Burlington was their destination because Adna's aunt was their sponsor and had been living in Burlington since 1997.

As they had done in Berlin, Adna and her sister, now 9 and 11, quickly adapted to a new life, this time in Burlington. Adna's parents were pleased that the school administrators here, in contrast with their German counterparts, strongly encouraged the family not to speak English at home. The thinking was that since the girls would be taught English at school, at home they should use their mother tongue, thus preserving access to their Bosnian heritage. This worked out as envisioned, and today Adna and Dzeneta are fluent in Bosnian, English and German. Through their professional careers and schooling, they have added to their language repertoire with the inclusion of French, Bahasa Indonesian and some Korean.

After completing Burlington High School, Adna attended the University of Vermont, majoring in Community International Development and minoring in French. While in school, Adna was employed at Burlington's Church Street Marketplace. Post-graduation, she was promoted to be the marketing manager. After three enjoyable years there, she enrolled at Cornell University, receiving her master's degree in city and regional planning with a focus on international planning and urban development in underdeveloped countries. She then worked at the World Resources

Joyfull, Dreamstime

Vegetable market in Banja Luka, Bosnia, August 2014.

Institute Ross Center for Sustainable Cities (WRI) in Washington, D.C. At WRI she worked on urban development projects and research focusing on equity, inclusiveness and paratransit in African cities. Today, Adna lives in Seoul, South Korea, and works at the World Smart Sustainable Cities Organization where the focus is on the advent and feasibility of including Information, Communication and Technology (ICT) in cities.

Adna's father works for the State of Vermont in the Agency of Transportation. He is also a highly ranked ping-pong player and has been Vermont state champion several times. Her mother worked for the Burlington School District and Fletcher Allen Hospital for many years and is now retired. Clearly Adna has adapted to life in America: she has received a solid education, and she has an excellent job and many friends. But her reflections below shed light on the lasting effects of the refugee experience.

> Once you get to another country, you are kind of stripped of everything. Whatever you might have known from your other country, your literature, your architecture, your whatever, no longer matters. When you've been through that experience you are at ground zero. Which is why I think that, no matter what, refugees always have more in common with each other than anyone else. I had more in common with a girl from the Sudan, at Cornell, than a girl from Croatia (who is not a refugee) because when you go through that experience you lose everything, your identity, your country, your language, everything. If somebody would ask me, what nationality I am, I would say "refugee," for the rest of my life.

Today, 20 years after the war, visiting Bosnia and Banja Luka is relatively routine and reasonably safe. Adna has been back several times but notes that life has not returned to the way it was when her family lived there. Although Adna does not have many memories of Banja Luka, she notices the stark difference between life in Republika Srpska and the Federation. One could say that ethnic cleansing is ongoing, as the systematic "Serbification" of every aspect of life in Banja Luka continues. Rebuilding of mosques is bitterly contested; streets and buildings have been renamed and the Cyrillic script is the prevalent form of writing, Thus Burlington, Vermont, for example, would be written *бурлингтон, Вермонт*. Ethnic slurs and threatening graffiti are not uncommon, and the pervasive, ongoing Serbian resistance to accepting the equal status of Muslims is a fact of life.

Katie Figura

IIII

ALMA MUJEZINOVIC

BOSNIA

Alma's first home in America was Middlebury, Vermont. She arrived here in 1998 as an 18-year-old, fluent in German and the language of her home country, Bosnian, but speaking very little English. She relates that life here was pleasantly different from the anti-foreigner climate she had experienced in Germany:

> My first impression was that people were always smiling and saying "hi" when they passed you on the street, even if they didn't know you. That was weird, but nice! School was hard because of my lack of English as well as lack of knowledge about the social system in school. As a teen that is kind of the most important thing.

Alma did very well academically, and, after finishing high school in two years, attended Massachusetts College of Art, in Boston, receiving a BFA in fashion in 2004.

Six years prior to arriving in Middlebury, Alma and her family had fled their home in Bosnia. They were from Prijedor, capital of one of the regions most severely affected by the Bosnian War. With the takeover of Prijedor in 1991 by Serb government and military forces, an intense program of scaremongering hate-filled propaganda, combined with the removal of non-Serbs from positions of power, set the stage for atrocities based on ethnicity: arbitrary killings, concentration camps and one of the worst massacres—approximately 3,000 civilians were killed—during the entire war. Croatians and Bosnian Muslims, like Alma and her family, were the main focus of this rage.

Alma's father was a truck mechanic, and after the takeover of Prijedor by Serbian forces, he was conscripted to work on their vehicles. He was picked up by two Serb soldiers every morning, taken to a garage to work on vehicles belonging to Serb forces and returned home by the soldiers in the evening. While the predictability of this routine was perhaps comforting, her dad knew that as soon as the Serbs brought in their own mechanics, in the best case he would no longer have a job, and in the worst case he would be sent to a concentration camp.

As the intensity of the conflict increased, Bosnian Muslims like Alma and her family began leaving Prijedor. Convoys of busses were deployed to evacuate both Bosniak (a term for Bosnian Muslims) and Croatian families. But leaving Prijedor by convoy was a dangerous enterprise; many were ambushed, resulting in the worst imaginable outcomes. On a tip from a friend, Alma's family took a more indirect, less-traveled route and reached the border without incident.

At the border, they walked across the bridge into Croatia, but were still far from safe. Joining others who had been waiting for days at a nearby gathering area, they were stoned by locals as they drove onward toward their goal, Zagreb, Croatia's capital. They were dropped off on the outskirts of Zagreb and left to their own devices to make the final push to safety. The surprise appearance of Alma's mother's uncle, a member of the Croatian army, and well-armed, saved the day. Accompanied by him, they had the confidence to approach the key checkpoint separating them and Zagreb. Once inside Zagreb, they spent a few weeks getting their papers in order before continuing to Germany, where they were to spend the next six years.

During the Bosnian War (1992–1995), Germany granted temporary residency to thousands of Bosnian Muslims fleeing the fighting, and for six years, the Bavarian city of Nuremberg was home for Alma's family. The girls learned German, made friends and attended public school, and both parents were able to find work to support their family. In the German education system, high school (known as "Gymnasium" in Germany) is

The important Islamic cultural site of Pocitelj, Hajji Alija's mosque, badly damaged during the Bosnian War, is now permanantly protected.

the normal path for preparing to go to college or university. At that time, refugees were not allowed to attend Gymnasium, so Alma took the only option available to her, vocational school, and studied fashion. As it turned out, her background in fashion has served her well.

Several years after the war ended, the German government terminated the temporary residency program, and the choice for Bosnian refugees was to return to Bosnia or apply for resettlement in a third country. At that time, with relations between the warring parties far from settled, returning to their former home in Bosnia was not appealing to Alma's family, probably

Alma Mujezinovic

Blagag Tekke, on the Buna River, one of Bosnia-Herzegovina's holiest sites.

unsafe. When their application to immigrate to Canada was denied, Alma's parents applied to the United States and were accepted. They had applied to Canada first, believing that Canada would be more likely to accept them.

Alma graduated from Massachusetts College of Art, and in 2005, newly married and looking for a change from life in Boston, Alma and her husband, Amer, decided to move to New York City. They enjoyed three productive years in New York, where Alma worked as a designer of women's clothing. When they decided to start a family, Alma and Amer returned to Burlington, confident that Vermont would be a better place to raise children. Today they have two sons, Hamza, eight, and Faris, six. Amer, who is also a Bosnian refugee, is a business analyst at the University of Vermont.

After returning to Vermont, Alma worked for the Burlington Housing Authority for eight years, where she worked with adults with disabilities.

She has recently transitioned to a different area of wellness care, childbirth. She now works as a prenatal and postnatal trainer, as well as a birth and postpartum doula, and loves her work.

In August 2018, Adna and her family traveled to Bosnia on vacation, visiting her grandmothers in Prijedor, now a very changed city. Bosnia—the country's formal name is Bosnia–Herzegovina—is comprised today, post-war, of two sub-states of essentially equal area: the Federation of Bosnia and Herzegovina and the Republika Sprska, RS for short. This equal-area partitioning was part of the Dayton Peace Accords, the war-ending peace agreement. Today the RS is overwhelmingly Serb, while the Federation is majority Bosniak (Bosnian Muslim) and Croat. These two entities are joined in a tense union, forming the country of Bosnia–Herzegovina. Prior to the Bosnian War the main ethnic groups of the region—Bosnian Muslim, Serb and Croat—were more or less evenly distributed throughout Bosnia–Herzegovina, but since the war a pronounced concentration of ethnic groups in "their" respective regions has taken place, an unfortunate state of affairs for those whose home areas are now dominated by an ethnic group different from their own. This has fallen hard on Alma and her family, as their hometown Prijedor is now in Serb-controlled Republika Sprska. Alma reflects on this:

When I first got there this summer [2018], although I had been back [to Bosnia] three times before, it hit me that the hometown I thought was my hometown no longer belonged to me. It didn't feel like a hometown you go back to. The people are completely different, it's a completely new population. It's people who have resettled there and I don't feel like I belong there. It was a very unusual feeling: I felt like a stranger in a place that feels really familiar. We traveled to other places in Bosnia for a few weeks, then came back and it felt a little better, but I knew it was no longer my place.

Despite feeling no longer at home in the city she is from, neither Alma nor Amer has a desire to sever ties with Bosnia. Alma was particularly struck by Bosnia's beautiful landscapes and its traditional architecture: she especially enjoys the laid-back European lifestyle. After their recent visit, Amer and Alma are thinking of buying an investment property in Bosnia. Amer tends toward Sarajevo, while Alma is more partial to a place in a rural setting.

❙❙❙❙

Kenan and Slavojka Avdibegovic

BOSNIA

Slavojka grew up on a farm in Doboj, Bosnia. One of four sisters, she describes her early life as a calm, beautiful childhood. She was born in 1967, and during most of her childhood her father lived and worked in Germany, while her mother took care of their modest family farm. As a result of Germany's almost complete loss of working-age men by the end of World War II, millions of men from southern Europe—Spain, Italy, Yugoslavia—worked there as "guest workers." In Germany they were able to earn more money than in their home countries, and many worked long enough to earn pensions. Slavojka's father was one of these guest workers, and the money he, and his compatriots, sent home had a significant impact on the Bosnian economy.

Two years after completing high school, Slavojka graduated from culinary school. Her first job was at a hotel in the town of Samac, about an hour from her hometown. Samac is nestled in the Sava River Valley, with Croatia directly across the river, and Serbia only a short distance away. As it happened, a local man by the name of Kenan was the director of the hotel, and the two of them soon fell in love, she a Serb, he a Muslim. While mixed marriages were very common in Samac, and throughout Bosnia, Slavojka's father was strenuously opposed to his daughter marrying a Muslim. But

Dreamstime

Bosnian village of Pocitelj.

marry they did—no one from her family attended the wedding—and for the next three years her father refused to see her, relenting only once, when war seemed imminent. Kenan and Slavojka were married in 1988, and a year later, with Kenan's help, Slavojka opened her own restaurant. Their son Zlatan was born in 1989. Life was good. In Slavojka's words: *When I think about it, it was a dream job, a dream life.*

In 1991, Croatia declared its independence from the Yugoslav Federation. Serbia, Croatia's neighbor to the east, responded by attacking Croatia, and by the following spring, what we now know as the Bosnian War was under way. Although the fighting was nearby—you could hear artillery fire in the distance—most residents of Samac felt this conflict, a war fueled by ethnic hatred and Serb nationalism, wouldn't affect them directly. After all, they lived in Bosnia, a model of multi-ethnic coexistence and religious tolerance. But as it turned out, they were wrong, terribly wrong. Early on in the conflict, Serbian forces took control of strategic border towns like Samac, and all able-bodied men, whether Serb or not, were forced to either join the army or help the Serb effort in some way. For Kenan, as a Muslim, this meant a life of forced labor, digging trenches for Serb soldiers at the frontline or helping to remove the contents from homes seized and plundered by Serbs: televisions, furniture, anything of value. He was gone for days at time, returning home exhausted and profoundly upset by gruesome sights he had witnessed. On one occasion Kenan and his crew avoided being shot by the thinnest of margins. They had been sent to empty the contents of a recently seized house and found the murdered bodies of the residents still there. Concerned that this "detail" would come to light, the Serb soldiers lined up Kenan and his fellow unfortunates against a wall, but intervention by a sympathetic Serb saved them from execution.

Kenan and Slavojka still lived in their apartment, but under miserable circumstances: food shortages, no running water and no electricity. And they struggled to keep themselves warm during winter nights. Kenan's hotel, where he had worked his entire career, had been taken over by Serb soldiers, and Slavojka's restaurant was looted, then destroyed. One December night, as they relaxed next to their woodstove, two-year-old Zlatan playing on the floor at their feet and Kenan's mother sitting on the couch next to them, they heard the familiar, distant "boom" of artillery—from across the river in Croatia—just two rounds.

When Slavojka came to, they were half-buried in debris. Both artillery shells had come through their roof, half-destroying their building. A brick wall had fallen on them, and the ceiling and the floor in the next room had collapsed. Dazed, she stared up at the sky through the open roof as snow fell around her. Their kitchen and bedroom were on fire, and light from the flames helped her see as she frantically dug in the rubble. She quickly found their son, covered in blood, but only slightly hurt. As she turned to free Kenan from the debris, he asked as he touched his legs: *What's this stuff?* From that moment, 28 years ago, he has been a paraplegic, paralyzed from the waist down. Slavojka was then 25 years old, Kenan was 41. As firemen put out the fires in their building, Slavojka blacked out and woke up later in the emergency room. Only slightly injured, she was able to return to their apartment the next day, and she discovered they had lost everything. The fire destroyed whatever possessions had survived the blast. Kenan had been taken that same night to a hospital in Belgrade, the Serbian capital, about three to four hours away, where he was to remain for three months. There, to the credit of his Serbian doctors, he received excellent treatment for his broken spine. During his hospital stay Slavojka was able to visit him, as she and Zlatan had moved in with her sister who lived 60 miles from Belgrade. She settled into a routine of alternating each grueling daylong trip to the hospital—two hours by bus each way—with a day of rest.

But when Kenan was released from the hospital and sent to a rehab facility, their situation took a turn for the worse. Imagine: you are unable to walk or even stand, and you are placed together with angry, wounded, drunk enemy soldiers who detest you, and who wouldn't think twice about killing you. Slavojka was so terrified she refused to leave Kenan's bedside for three days. She put their baby on Kenan's bed and huddled in a chair next to them. As a Serb herself, she was able to defuse the threatening atmosphere somewhat. By sheer luck it turned out that the representative for the hospitalized Serb soldiers was a musician who had played at Kenan's hotel before the war, and he was able to intervene and guarantee Kenan's safety.

After only two weeks in rehab, they were moved to the nearby UN refugee camp in Mataruska Banja, a defunct spa resort in southern Serbia. They lived there for three and a half years and with no prospects for the future other than survival. This was the lowest point in their lives. In Slavojka's words:

> You live normal life. Suddenly you are nobody. Yesterday everybody knows you, knows about you. Next day you are no one. You are low, below low.

They were housed in a 30-room villa and were allotted a small room with two beds and a sink—a single bathroom served the needs of the hundred residents. The food was minimal but adequate, although Slavojka had to get a doctor's prescription in order to obtain milk for Zlatan. As Kenan and Slavojka were the only ethnically mixed couple in the camp, visiting dignitaries were invariably brought to see them, since their existence in the camp offered "proof" of the false claim that Serbia was in fact ethnically and religiously tolerant.

Eventually they obtained a wheelchair—an ancient, monstrously heavy thing—and Slavojka was finally able to take Kenan outside into the fresh air. One day, as they strolled about, idly looking at vendor carts—they had no money to buy anything—they ran into a man who remembered Kenan from college. This fellow and his wife set in motion the necessary paperwork for Kenan and Slavojka to apply for immigration to the United States. Their application was approved, and in September of 1996, about a year after the war ended, the three of them, Zlatan was then seven, flew to St. Louis to start their new life in America. It bears mentioning that while Slavojka and her family were able to escape the dead-end refugee camp existence, today, 23 years later, war refugees still languish in that rundown villa in southern Serbia.

Belgrade, capital of Serbia.

Their difficulties were not over yet. Kenan's untreated kidney stone condition became critical just as they left Serbia. In the extreme agony that kidney stones inflict, Kenan's flight to the U.S. and his first several days here were unrelenting torture. This time, luck in the form of complete stranger—a fellow Bosnian and longtime U.S. resident—heard about Kenan's condition and spoke up for them. Over the objections of the local refugee agency—having just arrived here, Kenan was not yet officially registered as a U.S. resident—their newfound friend got Kenan admitted to Barnes Jewish Hospital, where doctors immediately operated, probably saving his life. In July of 1997, after Kenan recovered from bladder transplant surgery, they moved to Burlington to be closer to relatives already living here.

Today Slavojka is a lab supervisor for custodial services at the University of Vermont and loves her job. The ten people reporting to her come from nine different countries. Kenan takes care of things in their home in Burlington's New North End and gets up at 3:30 a.m. to prepare Turkish-style coffee for their morning ritual, a calm time of togetherness. Slavojka arrives at work by 5 a.m., and when she returns home in the early afternoon, they repeat their coffee ritual and reflect on the day's events.

John Hadden, Resting Lion Studio

The sub-states comprising Bosnia–Herzegovina as agreed in the Dayton Peace Accords, showing the Serb-controlled region (red) and the Muslim and Croat region (green).

Kenen and Slavojka have a lot of friends here, both American and Bosnian, and 22 members of their extended families live in the Burlington area. Kenan has three siblings here, a brother in Denmark and a sister in Serbia. Their son Zlatan, now in his mid-twenties, no longer lives at home and has graduated from UVM, majoring in computer science. He is fluent in his mother tongue and speaks Serbo-Croatian with his parents. When they first arrived here and Zlatan was starting school, although he spoke almost no English, Zlatan's teachers understood what the family had been through from Zlatan's drawings. Kenan and Slavojka love hunting for antiques and enjoy visiting Quechee and Montreal, and every summer they look forward to their annual beach vacation in Hampton, New Hampshire.

In their 22 years here, they have been back to Bosnia four times, visiting Doboj, where Slavojka's father and two of her sisters live. Her father lives on the family farm and continues to receive his monthly retirement check from Germany. Her mom died during the war of a heart attack. Kenan and Slavojka still own their now-rebuilt apartment in Samac, but since Kenan's mother died, it has been unoccupied.

Reflecting on what life is like in Bosnia, they observe that it is still a place where Muslims, Serbs and Croats coexist, but now, unlike pre-war days, each ethnic group tends to concentrate in its own area, as shown on the map. And there is no place for mixed couples such as themselves. According to Slavojka: *You won't be attacked, but you will never get a job.* Asked what they like about Burlington and Vermont, her response is: *Gosh, what we don't like! We like everything. We won't go back, even in a dream.*

HONG YU

CHINA

Hong Yu is one of our best-known immigrants; she is Burlington's very popular "dumpling lady." Hong was born in Shenyang, the regional capital of Liaoning. Liaoning is the province of China that lies just northeast of Beijing and borders North Korea. When she was very young, her family moved to Yingkou, a coastal city on the North China Sea, and this is where she grew up. Her father was an officer in the army and her mother worked in an office. Her childhood was comfortable, and in school she was a happy, bright child who loved singing and dancing. She performed often in school plays and performances.

While Hong's family was loving and supportive, it was also extremely strict by American standards. In her words, her father was like a "king," and all the kids feared his temper. When he was finished eating, the rest of the family immediately got up from the table and began clearing the dishes. If he wasn't home for dinner, the family didn't eat; and when guests came to visit, the kids were expected to wait on them. But her father was also an engaged and positive force in their lives. He particularly enjoyed his daughters' home performances with Hong singing and her sister on the violin. He had been a career military man for many years, and after he was killed

Hong (left), age 18, in Tiananmen Square with her sister.

in a motorcycle accident—Hong was 18 at the time—the family was able to maintain their standard of living on his pension.

While she was growing up, Hong remembers her teachers telling her how beautiful and wonderful America was. As a result, she always dreamed of coming here one day. In Chinese, the name for America happens to be "may kwaa," which translates as "beautiful country."

Years later, as a divorced parent of a young daughter, Hong decided to follow that dream. She had family in the United States, so why not give it a try? She moved to Buffalo, where her brother was working as a tour guide for Chinese visitors to Niagara Falls. Then after a year, in 1997, she moved to Burlington, where she has lived ever since. In Hong's words:

Before I became the Dumpling Lady, I worked as a housekeeper at a local hotel. One day I went to a Chinese restaurant in Burlington and ordered some dumplings, but unfortunately the taste was nothing compared to what I remembered: let's just say it was not on the good side. I learned how to cook when I was ten years old and the first thing I learned how to make was dumplings because my grandma lived with us and dumplings were her favorite food. Also both my mother and father loved dumplings. It was a family experience for me because we all made dumplings together on a huge table at home while having the best time. Those are some of my most fond memories.

After this experience I had a new goal. I wanted to bring my family recipe to life so the people of Burlington can have the same wonderful experience I had while I was growing up. So the rest is history. I love Burlington because they are some of the most positive, simple and kind people I have ever encountered in my life.

For the first two or three years, selling dumplings from a vendor cart on Church Street was not a success. Day after day she would return home with unsold food and simply throw it away, only to try again the next day. *She's very tough and doesn't give up easily*, recalls her husband, Doug. Her perseverance paid off: her dumpling cart became a big hit, and over the

Hong (second from left) with her daughter (second from right) and friends on a visit to China.

Jared Gange

Hong cooking dumplings at her cart on Church Street.

Katie Figura

Hong's famous dumplings.

17 years she ran it, she won *Seven Days'* Daisy for Best Food Vendor seven times.

Following a successful crowdfunding effort, Hong was able to transition from food cart to restaurant in November of 2017. Hong's Dumplings is located on the corner of Pearl and Pine Streets, just west of the Burlington Post Office. Business is great—she's hired several employees—and the restaurant is open year-round: she and her customers are no longer at the mercy of the weather. While her location has changed, the public's opinion of her dumplings has not: last year, in 2018, Hong won the *Seven Days'* Daisy for Best Dumplings.

Hong reflects on her relationship with China, Vermont and getting older:

Now that I am getting older, the most I miss about China is Chinese style home cooking, the food I grew up eating. I go back to China every four to five years for about two weeks to visit family and friends. I believe I will retire in Burlington because I absolutely love everything about this state; it has become an emotional attachment for me. Doug and I speak English to each other. I don't speak perfect English but we understand each other very well.

中国

DEMOCRATIC REPUBLIC of CONGO

with Burundi and Rwanda

The Democratic Republic of Congo is a land of enormous potential and mind-boggling tragedy. Straddling the equator and sitting squarely in the heart of Africa, the DRC, or DR Congo, or Congo, as it is variously known, is the second-largest country in Africa and almost four times the size of Texas. Its vast rainforest is second in size only to the Amazon, and Lake Tanganyika, on its eastern border, contains over 700 times the amount of water of Lake Champlain, almost as much as the five Great Lakes combined. Congo is fabulously rich in natural resources—it has significant reserves of diamonds, gold, cobalt, uranium, coltan, copper and tin—yet its people are among the poorest, by some measures *the* poorest, in the world. It's a sad fact that Congo's great natural wealth has also been its curse.

In 1960, after 50 years of rule, a period considered one of the most violent, repressive and exploitive colonial regimes in history, Belgium hurriedly granted Congo independence. But with essentially no trained civil servants—there were reportedly only three Congolese employed in the Belgian administration of over 5,000—the country was completely unprepared for self-governance. It's fair to say that even the best of leaders would have had a slim chance of overcoming the problems that arose. After independence was achieved, several key provinces immediately seceded, the Belgians assumed they would effectively retain control of the country and powerful multi-national corporations were determined to continue plundering the country's wealth.

The 35-year-old independence activist Patrice Lumumba was elected prime minister in a nationwide election, and his countrymen rejoiced in the dream of a prosperous, democratic future. This was not to be. Lumumba, admired in Africa today as a pan-African visionary who had his countrymen's interests at heart rather than his own, lasted only two months in office. Western governments, including the United States, kept a close eye on developments in mineral-rich Congo, and Lumumba was soon viewed as a problem in need of a solution. The Cold War was at its height in 1960, and Lumumba's overtures to the Soviet Union for help—after initial requests for assistance to the UN and the United States were

Scene from the Congolese city of Goma, on the border with Rwanda.

ignored—were seen as extremely dangerous. Placed under house arrest, he later escaped, but was subsequently captured, brutally tortured, executed by firing squad and his body dismembered and dissolved in acid. Thus, seven months after his popular election, the "problem" of Africa's first modern leader was solved.

A power struggle ensued, as various factions vied for supremacy. By 1965, Mobutu Seko, who had been Lumumba's Army Chief of Staff, had succeeded in gaining control of the country. Sophisticated, cunning and favored by the West for his anti-communist stance, Mobutu managed to stay in power for 32 years, all the while accumulating vast personal wealth and vigorously suppressing dissenting elements. According to the British journalist, Michela Wrong:

> No other African president had been presented with a country of such potential yet achieved so little. No other leader had plundered his economy so effectively or lived the high life to such excess.

Mobutu built a $100 million palace in his home village, Gbadolite, far from Kinshasa, Congo's capital. It is said that a Mercedes fleet met his

100-person entourage when it was flown in to lavish parties at the jungle retreat. Shopping trips to New York and Paris necessitated flying by the supersonic Concorde, to save time. Should he tire of Gbadolite, he could drop in on his mansion in Switzerland, one of his villas in Spain or Portugal or his apartment in Paris. His kleptocratic rule is unparalleled in Africa.

The country's mineral wealth, valued in the trillions of dollars, found (and continues to find) ready markets throughout the world, ensuring a flow of money other countries in the region could only dream of. While Mobutu's family members and his cronies were enriched, and regional governors were placated by cash payoffs, the average Congolese benefitted little. For those opposing, or even appearing to oppose, the regime, torture and murder were the government's response. Mobutu's human rights record is one of the worst in Africa.

Unfortunately, in the years after Mobutu's rule, and up to the present, the prospects for most Congolese have not improved—for many, they have

John Haddon, Resting Lion Studio

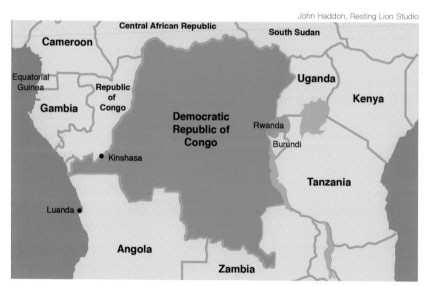

The Democratic Republic of Congo is approximately four times the size of Texas.

TEXAS

68

Living conditions in a refugee camp, Democratic Republic of Congo.

worsened. The successor governments have also been corrupt, although not on the scale of Mobutu. Of great relevance to the issue of refugees, and internally displaced persons, is the fact that Kinshasa is on one side of the country, and the mineral-rich provinces are on the other (eastern) side of the country. Since there is no reliable road connection through the 1,500 miles of jungle separating east from west, this separation is easily exploited by rebel groups in the eastern part of the country. As a consequence, lack of personal safety, forced labor and the absence of basic services are facts of life in eastern Congo. Rape and sexual mutilation are widespread: The DRC is known as the Rape Capital of the World, and according to the UN Refugee Agency (UNHCR), at the end of 2017 there were 4.5 million internally displaced persons in the Democratic Republic of Congo.

But as inhumane, unfair and cruel as the circumstances described above are, in 1994 an event took place in the tiny neighboring country of Rwanda that was much worse. The aftereffects are still playing out today. In fact this event is the major reason for the prescence of Congolese and Rwandan refugees in the United States and elsewhere, as well as for the seemingly intractable problem of the destabilization of eastern Congo.

Rwanda

Located on the eastern border of Congo, tiny Rwanda is today a stabile, safe and relatively prosperous country. From the tourism perspective, Rwanda is best known for its world-famous mountain gorillas. Blessed with stupendous natural beauty, fertile soils and a pleasant tropical climate, Rwanda is about the size of Vermont, but with 20 times the population. Most of the population consists of subsistence farmers who live in the hilly lowlands. Sometimes referred to as the land of a thousand hills, Rwanda's densely populated hills are essentially distinct villages, each with its own municipal administration. Uganda borders Rwanda to the north and Tanzania to the east. Burundi, similar to Rwanda in size, population and ethnicity, lies just to the south. The relationship between Rwanda and the Congolese provinces of North and South Kivu, which lie west and south of Rwanda is discussed below.

Like Congo, Rwanda was a Belgian colony, and in 1962, two years after granting Congo independence, Belgium granted independence to Rwanda. But Rwanda was, and is, a very different place from Congo. In particular, without significant mineral wealth, Rwanda had not been coveted and exploited by external interests to the extent Congo had been.

Rwanda's problems are internal, one could almost say personal. Two ethnic groups, the majority Hutu and the minority Tutsi, together account for about 99% of the population. While there are about six times as many Hutus as Tutsis, historically Tutsis made up Rwanda's ruling class. This class distinction was strengthened during the colonial period, as first the Germans, and then the Belgians, favored the cattle-owning Tutsis over the Hutu farmers, believing the former to be the superior group. As a result, Tutsis received better opportunities for jobs and education. Curiously, there is very little physical difference between the two groups, with some scholars rejecting the claim that Hutus and Tutsis are in fact distinct ethnic groups. The popular generalization is that Tutsis are taller, their facial features smaller and more angular and their women more attractive.

In any event, with independence came the understandable Hutu demand for proportional representation in the government. As the majority Hutus gained control of the country, the stage was set for the settling of old scores, the exacting of revenge and, more generally, efforts by Hutus to excise their feelings of inferiority toward Tutsis. The end result was a bloodbath the likes of which has not been seen in modern times.

Typical Rwandan hill farm setting.

In the years following independence, persecution of Tutsis by the increasingly dominant Hutus led many Tutsis to flee to neighboring Uganda. In 1990, an invasion by a well-organized Uganda-based Tutsi army triggered a civil war in Rwanda that lasted until 1993. The uneasy peace that ensued was shattered on April 6, 1994, when the plane carrying Rwanda's Hutu president was shot down over the capital, Kigali. It has never been determined who was responsible, but Hutus blamed the Tutsis, and extremist Hutu elements immediately set in motion a suspiciously well-prepared, countrywide attack on Tutsis. In Kigali, Tutsi officials and Hutu moderates in positions of power were murdered within hours of the plane crash.

Over the course of next three months, Hutu extremists—known as *genocidaires*—and their followers set about their grim task. For the most part, using only machetes and clubs, they methodically slaughtered approximately 800,000—perhaps as many as a million—Tutsi men, women and children. This amounted to 10% of the country's population, and perhaps two-thirds of all Rwandan Tutsis. Put into perspective, this is

Dreamstime

Skulls of Genocide victims, Rwandan Genocide Memorial.

more than were killed in America's four-year-long Civil War, and over a period of only three months. This event, known as the Rwandan Genocide, defies understanding.

Two very similar groups of people, living among each other as neighbors, as friends, as teachers and as inter-married couples, were suddenly at war with each other. But this was no war. This was a carefully planned program to eradicate an entire ethnic group—genocide, pure and simple. While Hutu-extremist paramilitary units ordered and directed the genocide, the killing was primarily carried out by everyday people. Day after day, week after week, Hutu villagers went out with machetes and clubs, hunted down and killed their neighbors, their friends, their teammates and their teachers, because they were Tutsi. Moderate Hutus unwilling to join in the killing were also eliminated. Astoundingly, some Hutu men married to Tutsi women killed their wives—and in some cases their own children, simply because they resembled their Tutsi mothers. The killers referred to this activity as "going to work," and they nearly succeeded in their goal of eliminating all Tutsis. As an indication of the magnitude of participation, in Rwanda today approximately 100,000 men, and some women, remain imprisoned—convicted, or awaiting trial—for their roles in the slaughter.

The outside world was slow to react to events in Rwanda, despite repeated warnings and calls for help. In fact, aside from some involvement from France, outside help was essentially nonexistent. By the time Western governments acknowledged that a genocide was taking place, it was largely over. President Bill Clinton and Madeline Albright, our ambassador to the UN at the time, have apologized to the people of Rwanda for our country's inaction.

In the Democratic Republic of Congo, the Hutu–Tutsi divide has historically not been a significant factor. However, one could argue that the Rwandan Genocide had a greater effect on Congo than on Rwanda: the problems it spawned are still playing out in Congo, over 25 years later.

Why was Congo so profoundly affected? During the months of the genocide, Tutsi-led forces (the Rwandan Patriotic Front, the RPF) gradually gained control of Rwanda. As it became clear that the RPF would succeed in retaking the country, Hutus—both perpetrators and non-participants— fearing reprisals, streamed out of Rwanda into Burundi, Tanzania and eastern Congo. Tutsis who had not already fled abandoned their homes as the remaining Hutu killers redoubled their efforts in the final days of the genocide. Thus, in a very short span of time, Congo found itself host to an estimated two million refugees, victims and perpetrators alike.

International aid groups established camps for the refugees in eastern Congo near the Rwandan border, and Tutsis and Hutus once again found themselves living in close contact, as the foreign aid workers were unable to distinguish Hutu from Tutsi. Hutus, many of whom had taken part in the genocide, could reorganize without interference and, by selling donor-supplied food and medical supplies, buy weapons and nurse their goal of regaining control of Rwanda.

By 1996, the new Tutsi-dominated government of Rwanda, frustrated by the unresolved and threatening refugee situation just across the border, invaded Congo. The goal was to bring perpetrators of the genocide to justice and bring victims and other non-belligerents back to their villages. Within seven months the RPF had returned most Rwandans home and deposed President Mobutu, ending his dictatorial rule. This incursion triggered the First Congo War; it was followed a year later by the Second Congo War. This second war, involving seven neighboring countries (including Angola, Zimbabwe and Uganda), took the lives of somewhere between four and six million Congolese. As such, it is the deadliest conflict since World War II.

Unfortunately, when the Rwandan army disbanded the refugee camps, Hutu extremists escaped and have been able to survive by preying on the local Congolese population. The situation in the region has evolved to the point where much of eastern Congo is lawless and unstable, with various rebel factions controlling different territories. Meanwhile, foreign corporations continue to benefit from the exploitive extraction of Congo's enormous mineral wealth, especially the mining of relatively rare minerals crucial to the production of electronic devices, cell phones in particular. Mining takes place in small operations in remote areas and is controlled by armed rebels, without oversight—forced labor and extremely dangerous working conditions are the norm. The minerals sought—cassiterite, gold, wolframite, columbite-tantalite among them—are referred to as conflict minerals, because the violent, uncontolled way they are obtained contributes to the prolongation of conflict. Congo's dysfunctional government is essentially irrelevant in this part of the country. Next door, Rwanda, under the firm control of Paul Kagame's government, enjoys peace, stability and generous Western support, while Congo, with its vast wealth and untapped human potential, is crippled by problems far beyond its ability to solve.

Burundi

Burundi is Rwanda's immediate neighbor to the south, and the DRC lies to the west. The northern tip of Lake Tanganyika forms the southern part of Burundi's border with Congo. Similar in size and population makeup to Rwanda, Burundi's political history also has a great deal in common with Rwanda's grave internal conflicts. Like Rwanda, Burundi is majority Hutu, with Tutsis constituting 10% to 15% of the population, and the Twa people—pygmies—making up about 1%. The primary language spoken in both countries is Kirundi, or a variation thereof. Swahili, the language of commerce in East Africa and French, a legacy of the French and Belgian colonial periods, are also widely spoken. Both countries are about 60% Catholic, also a legacy of French and Belgian missionaries, with the remainder adhering to indigenous beliefs.

The vast majority of Burundians, over 90%, are farmers, and the country has only one large city, Bujumbura (population 500,000 in 2008), the capital. Crops include beans, corn, sweet potatoes, cassava, bananas and coffee. The popular, inexpensive beer of the region is made from the fermentation of mashed bananas. Burundi's coffee is a major source of export revenue and can be found on supermarket shelves in the U.S. The country's wildlife—elephant, antelope, baboon, buffalo, hippo, crocodile—are a potential source of tourism revenue, but the country's meager resources are not up to

Children breaking up rocks to make gravel, Bujumbura, Burundi.

the task of providing necessary infrastructure or adequate protection from poaching. The diminishment of habitat—deforestation and the expansion of farming—brought about by the country's fast-growing population is a further hindrance to wildlife preservation.

Beyond the many benign similarities Rwanda and Burundi share, the ethnic rivalry—and extreme violence—between Tutsis and Hutus is unfortunately a major theme in Burundi as well. While lacking the notoriety of the Rwanda Genocide, Burundi has nevertheless experienced horrific episodes of violence. For example, during Burundi's civil war (1993–2005), a conflict driven by animosity between Hutus and Tutsis, an estimated 300,000 lives were lost.

Kyendamina "Cleophace" Mukeba

DEMOCRATIC REPUBLIC OF CONGO

On a July day in 1996, Cleophace's mother went to the market to buy food for her family, as she did every day. She never returned. Bernadette was tall and slender, with delicate features, and because of her appearance she was killed, in broad daylight, by a complete stranger. Her children who were at home at the time, Cleophace among them, were notified that they should come and get her body. She was buried that same day.

As shocking and inexplicable as it may seem, her murder was not random: she was a victim of an event that had played out in a neighboring country two years earlier, the Rwandan Genocide. The genocide in Rwanda was an attempt by the country's majority ethnic group, Hutus, to exterminate the minority ethnic group, the Tutsis. But as Tutsi forces gained control of Rwanda and stopped the genocide, thousands of Hutus, fearing prison or death, fled Rwanda to neighboring Congo (Zaire, as it was then known). There, personnel in the UN-monitored refugee camps, unable to make the distinction between Tutsi and Hutu, unwittingly allowed the two groups to live together. As eastern Congo was then, and is now, only nominally under government control, Hutu extremists could kill anyone they suspected of being Tutsi with little fear of reprisal. Thus, Congolese citizens like Bernadette, with no connection with Rwanda, but with Tutsi morphology—Tutsi appearance—were targeted by rogue Rwandan Hutus who had taken up residence in Congo. This complex issue is discussed in detail in the introductory section on Rwanda and Congo.

Cleophace comes from a large family—he has 22 siblings. His father had two wives, one in Congo, and another only a few miles away in neighboring Burundi. As was common among people in the region, he moved back and forth between the two countries. Cleophace, although Congolese, was born in Burundi. Cleophace's dad was a skilled tradesman, by turns a carpenter, welder and upholsterer, and was better able to support his family by working in Burundi than in his home country of Congo. In 1978, after the Burundian government expelled all Congolese from Burundi, Cleophace's father consolidated his large family in Congo. Despite many mouths to feed, Cleophace and his siblings got by and always had a roof over their heads, but as Cleophace relates, *Life was not easy, we lived in abject poverty. At times I ate only once every two or three days.* Cleophace was able to finish high school and begin college, but for a variety of reasons, primarily the lack of money for tuition, he was unable to complete his studies.

In October of 1996, the Rwandan army, pursuing the perpetrators of the genocide and determined to repatriate displaced Tutsis, invaded eastern Congo, scattering, capturing and killing thousands, and in the process, turning Cleophace's home turf into a war zone. Together with thousands of others, Cleophace and a younger brother fled south away from the conflict zone (see map). Meanwhile, as fate would have it, Cleophace's wife, Malinga, was on a business trip in neighboring Burundi, only 15 miles from their home. The borders were immediately sealed, and it was impossible—not to mention unsafe—for her to return home. Seven years would pass before the recently married couple saw each other again.

Although Burundi became a kind of prison for Malinga, she was out of harm's way and in a country familiar to her. Things were far more uncertain for Cleophace. His plan was to make his way from country to country, eventually reaching South Africa, and to live there until it was safe to return to Congo. Getting to South Africa turned out not to be possible; in fact he had difficulty traveling through his own country. His Tutsi-like appearance—tall and slender, like his mother—continually put him at risk. In one instance he was detained by soldiers, and before they would let him proceed, he had to prove he was an internally displaced, "real" Congolese, not a Rwandan refugee or soldier. His competency in the local language, Lega, saved the day.

Jared Gange

King and Amani take a break from shooting hoops on a hot August day, Burlington, 2018.

After he and his brother separated—on the theory that, by doing so, they increased the odds of at least one of them surviving—Cleophace secured passage across Lake Tanganyika to Tanzania. He then continued by boat south to Zambia and from there, by hitching rides, made it to neighboring Malawi, only to be detained and immediately returned to his starting point in Zambia. After four days in jail there, he was able to continue south in Zambia to the town of Kasama, where he was jailed for three weeks. From Kasama, his journey took him to Maheba, still in Zambia, where he and his fellow travelers spent two months in a refugee camp, enduring cramped, filthy conditions and starvation-level rations. From there, he hitched a ride to Lusaka, Zambia's capital, which, unknown to him at the time, was to be

Left to right, top to bottom: Bernadette, Cleophace, King, Nyota, Amani, Malinga.

his home for the next nine years. But instead of settling down, he continued toward South Africa and the stability and security it represented. Hitching rides with friendly truck drivers, he made it to Beira, in Mozambique, a small town on the Indian Ocean. But denied permission to continue south toward South Africa by the local authorities, he hitched north to Lilongwe, back in Malawi. Here he was taken in by local Seventh Day Adventists, who fed him and gave him shelter for two weeks. Finally, worn out by three months of travel and uncertainty, he set his sights on Lusaka, hoping to make a go of it there.

In Lusaka, he first worked at odd jobs, including as a street vendor, selling cigarettes. But eventually he found that his education—high school and some college—enabled him to find work as a tutor, and he gradually acquired enough students to support himself. He also began a determined search for his wife. Not daring to leave Zambia, he contacted the Red Cross to facilitate his search, but after the Red Cross was unable to locate her in their camps in Tanzania, Burundi, Uganda and Kenya, he turned to the network of Catholic churches in the region. Aware that many refugees were living in and around Kigoma (in Tanzania) Cleophace sent off a letter, addressing it to *Any Catholic Church in Kigoma*. This worked: Malinga was in Kigoma. By examining Cleophace's handwriting, Malinga was convinced that the person looking for her was in fact her husband. They started corresponding and finally, after almost seven years of separation, they were reunited in Lusaka in March of 2002.

As a tutor in Lusaka, Cleophace was able to support Malinga, allowing her to stay at home and take care of their baby daughter. After convincing the authorities they were man and wife, and bona fide refugees, they underwent an arduous interview process with the UNHCR (United Nations High Commissioner for Refugees), the Joint Voluntary Agency and finally the Immigration and Naturalization Service (now Department of Homeland Security). After six grueling interviews, spanning a period of three years, they were cleared to immigrate to America.

John Hadden, Resting Lion Studio

Cleophace's three-month-long failed attempt to reach safety in South Africa.

Ibutwa

Cleophace with women who receive help from his Ibutwa Initiative, Democratic Republic of Congo, 2015.

Cleophace and Malinga, with their daughter Bernadette (named after Cleophace's mother), were resettled in Burlington in 2005. When Cleophace first arrived here, he held various jobs at Fabtech, Green Mountain Coffee Roasters, UVM College of Medicine, Merchants Bank and Opportunities Credit Union. Determined to complete his education, he started out at CCV. Then after a semester at Champlain College, he received enough financial assistance (both merit-based and diversity-based) from St. Michael's College to complete his undergraduate degree there, majoring in Political Science. He continued his education at Vermont Law School, earning a master's degree in environmental law and policy in 2015. It wasn't until 2012—after an absence of fifteen years—that Cleophace was able to visit his home country, and then on a tourist visa, as a U.S. citizen with an American passport.

Today Cleophace, 52, is employed as an interpreter and tutor of French, Swahili and Lingala in the Winooski School District for students in elementary, middle and high school. With his fluency in these three important languages of Africa, and his excellent command of English, he is a valuable asset, facilitating good communication between the teachers and African students and their parents. Cleophace is a frequent speaker at St. Michael's College, Champlain College and for other groups, explaining to students and the general public the very difficult circumstances of people living in the Democratic Republic of Congo, in particular eastern Congo. Malinga is a nurse's aide at the Converse Home in Burlington. In the years Cleophace and Malinga have been in Burlington, they have added three children to their family: Tambwe King (born in 2006), Amani Gloire (2009) and Nyota Marie-Jeanne (2013).

Asked what his children like to do, Cleophace replies:

Bernadette loves academics more than anything, and she has a great voice for singing; King is more artistic, is a good dancer and sings in church; Amani is great in school, loves science and math and is good at basketball and tennis and wants to learn skating; Nyota, the youngest, loves dancing, reading and singing.

Cleophace's great passion, his mission in life, is to help women who are victims of the rape and sexual mutilation that are a fact of life in the ongoing violence and exploitation in South Kivu, the province of Congo where Cleophace is from.

Most women who are victims of rape are shunned by their communities and rendered homeless. In response to this, Cleophace has created a non-profit called the Ibutwa Initiative (www.ibutwa.org) that helps the women rebuild their lives. Ibutwa provides micro loans for small businesses, purchases farming plots, assists with medical expenses and pays for the school uniforms and tuition for the women's children. In the Congo there is no tax-based, publicly funded school system such as we have in this country, so teacher salaries and school facilities are funded by tuition fees. Cleophace is in almost daily phone contact with Ibutwa's employees in the field, and in 2015, he visited South Kivu to spend time working with the project participants and local staff.

Eva Sollberger for *Seven Days*

ROBERT ACHINDA

DEMOCRATIC REPUBLIC OF CONGO

Robert was born June 15, 1965, in Lubonja, in eastern Congo, in the province of South Kivu. At the time, the country was in great turmoil and Robert's family was fleeing the violence. Conditions were so dangerous that Robert was born when his family was on the run—in the bush—as Robert puts it. The Congo, then still known as the Belgian Congo, was divided into many small entities, and various groups were fighting each other for control of the country. Robert's father, a well-known political activist and the leader of one such group, had recently been killed, leaving his young family particularly vulnerable. Ironically, a man who worked closely with Robert's father at the time did eventually become the president of Congo: this complicated history is addressed in the introduction to the Democratic Republic of Congo.

The death of Robert's father led to the family being split up, as none of their relatives could manage to support the entire family. As a result, when Robert was two years old, he was sent to live with his grandfather, a bishop in the town of Kalimie, a small city on the shores of Lake Tanganyika. There he attended grade school and when it was time for him to go to high school, he moved to the northern city of Bukavu, close to Congo's border with Rwanda. He lived with his older brother and continued his schooling, completing all but the last year, when lack of money for tuition forced him to leave school.

He then moved in with "the big sister of my mother" in the lakeside city of Uvira, which is perched at the northern end of 400-mile-long Lake Tanganyika, the second-largest lake in the world by volume. Robert has happy memories of those days; walking down to Lake Tanganyika first thing in the morning, washing his face in the pure water before going home for his morning tea. Later he moved to his mom's village to dig for gold in an area of Congo that is home to one of Africa's richest goldfields. He did this for two to three years, made some money, discovered partying, drinking and girls. At this point his younger brother Richard intervened, warning him to be careful and not get a girl pregnant, because in Africa, as Robert recalls:

> If any girl say—even if she is lying—I am pregnant of Robert, what they do over there—they don't go to hospital to check—the family just bring that girl to your house and you have a wife. My brother was worried about that, so I stay away, far away from that. And to do that, I start working for God.

As a preacher, Robert found his calling and he soon found the woman he wanted to marry, Anna, also a preacher. They married in Uvira and Robert

Terry Allen

Robert's sister-in-law, Debbie Allen (his mother in Vermont), Robert and his mother Suzanne,

recalls that over a thousand people came to their wedding. Through their church—the Pentecostal Missionary Union of Great Britain and Ireland—Robert and Anna came to know many people. Nine happy years passed and they produced eight children. In this period Robert began to speak out on human rights, to speak for the voiceless, as he puts it. This did not sit well with the government. President Mobutu's regime was profoundly corrupt, and while matters of basic human rights did not register on Mobutu's radar, dissenting voices surely did.

About this time, in 1996, the First Congo War broke out. This was a direct result of the Rwandan army's pursuit of perpetrators of the Rwandan Genocide (1994) into Congo, destabilizing a country already overwhelmed by the presence of millions of refugees from Rwanda. Meeting little resistance, Rwandan soldiers walked accross the country—over a thousand miles—ultimately reaching the capital, Kinshasa. Here, Mobutu was quickly overthrown and none other than Laurent Kabila, Robert's father's activist colleague from 30 years before, was installed as president of the country.

Although the Democratic Republic of Congo, then known as Zaire, was neither a republic nor democratic, it was not cursed with the Tutsi–Hutu conflict that was the underlying reason for the Rwandan Genocide. However, Zaire's (Congo's) own small community of ethnic Tutsis, known as *Banyamulenge*, did come under threat. Zaire's leader, Mobutu, was pro-Hutu (Hutus were the perpetrators of the genocide), and as a result, the Banyamulenge living in eastern Congo found themselves in the same deadly predicament faced by Tutsis in Rwanda.

It is to Robert Achinda's great credit that he, a person with no tribal or family connection to the Banyamulenge, came to their defense. First attempting to work with local authorities to protect them, then secretly aiding in their escape from Congo, Robert eventually came under scrutiny himself. Tipped off that he was about to be arrested, Robert and his family, like many others displaced by the fighting, made the perilous voyage across Lake Tanganyika to safety in Kigoma, Tanzania. His comment about the 30-mile crossing in a flimsy boat: *You stay maybe you die. You cross, maybe you die or maybe you live. You decide. Lucky for us, the hurricane was sleeping.*

Anna and Robert quickly found their footing in Tanzania. Because of their renown as preachers, and partly because of Robert's work on behalf of the Banyamulenge, a house was made available to them, sparing them the miserable existence of life in a refugee camp. Soon they were preaching in two churches. But once again Robert felt the need to speak out, this time about the unhealthy, dangerous conditions in Kigoma's refugee camp: he complained to the local authorities and wrote letters to the UN.

About this time (2004) Robert traveled to Texas to a religious conference. While in Texas he got word that his safety couldn't be guaranteed if he returned to Tanzania, apparently because of his outspokenness about the plight of refugees. Thus began his eight-year struggle to gain asylum in the United States. After relocating to Boston and working with an Africa specialist and an immigration attorney who spoke Swahili, Robert was granted asylum status in 2013.

In the interim he had moved to Vermont and, after a stint working at Fanny Allen Heath Care as a custodian, started his own cleaning business. Thanks to the generosity of the local community, his entire family, including his mother, was able to join him in Hinesburg. He liked to say about Vermont: *The weather is cold, but the people are warm!*

Tragically, about the time he was granted permanent status here, he was diagnosed with pancreatic cancer. He enjoyed two years with his family before passing away in July 2015. His story, and his struggle with cancer, has been profiled by *Seven Days'* "Stuck in Vermont" series.

Jared Gange

Robert's wife and kids after a concert performance in Hinesburg, summer 2016.

Eva Sollberger for *Seven Days*

Robert and Anna preaching.

Robert is no longer with us, but his family is thriving. Anna is working as a preacher and the kids are all in school; the older ones have after-school jobs. The four oldest have graduated from Champlain Valley High School and are attending college in Burlington. The girls are talented singers and have performed locally.

In 2017, two years after Robert's death, Anna and the four youngest children moved to St. Louis, where Anna has taken a job as the lead minister in a new church. Anna is so highly regarded—even revered—as a preacher within African Pentecostal communities that several families from Boston and Vermont moved to St. Louis to be able to attend her sermons.

Robert's younger brother, Richard, is a high official in the administration of the Democratic Republic of Congo. He reflects on Robert's life:

Robert's life was truly rich, and I confirm that he had a great heart, full of compassion. Putting his own life in danger, he helped the Banyamulenge in Uvira. Robert was a man of peace who contributed to the 2009 Peace Conference in Kinshasa.

Pascal and his wife Justine.

IIIII

PASCAL NDIMURWANKO

BURUNDI

When Pascal arrived in Vermont from Africa on September 25, 2007, he was 42 years old. Thirty-five years earlier, in 1972, when he was seven, he and his family fled from their home to escape the murderous ethnic violence raging in Burundi. In this particular instance of ethnic violence—there have been many such instances in Burundi—members of the Tutsi ethnic group killed about 200,000 ethnic Hutus. Pascal and his family are Hutus, and they joined the many thousands of their Hutu brethren fleeing to the neighboring countries of Congo, Rwanda and Tanzania. Pascal's family was able to escape by crossing Lake Tanganyika to Congo (Democratic Republic of Congo), where there they lived for the next 23 years, never returning to Burundi, although they were never farther than a few hours' drive from the border.

Within our local frame of reference, it's as if some of us were driven out of Vermont (Burundi is slightly bigger than Vermont), escaped by boat across Lake Champlain to New York state and lived in tents and primitive huts in, say, Lake Placid, never daring to visit friends and family back home in Vermont.

When the fighting broke out in April of 1972, Pascal, his mother and three siblings left home under the cover of darkness to avoid detection

Justine and the "family car," refugee camp, Tanzania.

by the armed fighters, and almost certain death. Together with about 10 others, and accompanied by a couple of goats, they paddled a narrow, 25-foot dugout canoe across 20 miles of the unpredictable waters of Lake Tanganyika to Congo.

Once in Congo, they found safe haven in the lakeside town of Uvira. Ironically, Uvira is within walking distance (15 miles) of Burundi's capital, Bujumbura. After two years in Uvira, a United Nations refugee agency moved Pascal and his family to Malinde Refugee Camp, a few hours south, near the town of Baraka. This was his family's home for the next 22 years. Pascal was able to go to elementary school in the camp itself and went to nearby towns for high school. After high school, he was unemployed for a few years but eventually got a job teaching French and psychology at a school about seven hours' walk from the camp. He was paid in goats, one per month.

Meanwhile, his parents were able to obtain a small plot of land, located about a kilometer from Malinde, where they grew sweet potatoes, corn, bananas, beans and nutrient rich cassava, thus supplying the family's food needs after the UN rations ceased.

In 1995, Pascal married Justine Nyanzira, also a Burundian but born in Congo. As in Pascal's case, Justine's family had fled Burundi; however, they were forced out during an earlier episode of ethnic violence. Justine has been in Burundi only once, very briefly. It's important to note that while Congo was a safe haven for these Burundian families, it was nevertheless a foreign country for them, with a different language and a different culture. The language the two countries have in common is French, a legacy of French and Belgian colonial rule.

As limiting as their refugee camp existence was, it did provide a measure of peace and stability. But this peaceful, safe existence was shattered in 1996. War, and its attendant violence and chaos, came to the area of Congo where Pascal and his family lived, and once again, as Hutus, they found themselves targets of ethnic hatred. And once again they fled across Lake Tanganyika, but in a larger, safer boat, arriving this time in Tanzania, which is just south of Burundi. And, once again, their lot was a refugee camp, this time for 11 years.

In Tanzania, the UNHCR (UN High Commissioner for Refugees) provided them with tents and food. After the families settled in, they built simple shelters of sticks and mud (so-called wattle and daub construction), using the UN-supplied tent material to waterproof the roofs. They cooked their meals outside except when rains forced them inside, although this sometimes led to the huts catching fire. Their huts were tiny, affording no privacy. Pascal was able to earn a little money teaching in the camp's primary school. Eventually Pascal and his family managed to build a more substantial structure using mud bricks. The food provided by the UN, doled out every two weeks, was very basic—beans, rice, corn, cooking oil and salt—barely enough to survive on. Luckily, they were able to trade some of this food for fresh fish and vegetables. In 1997, their first child, Merci, was born. Today she is a junior at the University of Vermont.

In 2006, the United Nations placed Pascal on a list of candidates for possible relocation to the United States. In the screening process that followed, some of his relatives and friends passed, others did not. When the examiners asked him why he didn't want to return to his country of origin,

Burundi, he explained that he hadn't been there since he was seven, and for him to return, at age 42, to a country he no longer knew, to a country still dangerous for him, was not a viable option. Thus he, and his family, were cleared to emigrate to America. After some training (including how to use a flush toilet), Pascal, his wife, five children, his mother and sister-in-law left refugee camp existence behind and arrived in Burlington in September 2007.

Today Pascal and Justine work in housekeeping at the UVM Medical Center. They and their family, ten people in all, live in an upstairs apartment in Burlington's North End. All are now U.S. citizens, including Pascal's 80-year-old mother. When asked what he thinks of his existence here, he replies that he is happy for his kids and their future. His own options in terms of a career are more limited, but with their two incomes, at least their basic needs are taken care of. He would like to own his own home someday but at this point can't afford it. Their next oldest, 17-year-old Kennedy, at left in an earlier photo above, is headed to college next year.

Pascal's mom in Tanzania, before moving to America.

Pascal and Justine's son Kennedy with a friend.

To summarize, Pascal and his family, like many Burundian Hutus, were the victims of two conflicts; one could say they are "double" refugees. In the first instance they were forced to leave Burundi, and in the second instance many years later, they fled the Congo. It is an irony that while Tutsi were the perpetrators of the 1972 Burundian Genocide, it was Hutus who slaughtered Tutsis during the 1994 genocide in Rwanda. But Pascal lost on both counts. After the Rwandan Genocide, large numbers of Hutu perpetrators escaped to neighboring Congo, finding safe haven there. But in 1996, the Rwandan military invaded Congo in an attempt to bring these killers to justice. In the chaos that followed—known as the First Congo War—little distinction was made between Hutu extremists and innocent Hutus, and Hutus living in Congo near the Rwandan border found themselves in danger. Thus, once again, Pascal and his family were forced to flee for their lives.

Note: This interview was conducted in 2016. Pascal and his family have since moved to Kentucky.

96

ALDO IVAN CRUZ

ECUADOR

Ivan Cruz was born the oldest of three children in Quito, the capital of Ecuador. He and his two sisters were cared for by their grandmother during their early life, as their parents were living and working in the United States. His childhood was typical; he went to school, attended church and played in the city parks with his friends and cousins.

When he was 17, his parents brought him to New York City, to Queens. Queens is home to immigrants from all over the world, and many thousands of newcomers have started their life in the U.S. in Queens. The plan for Ivan was that he would attend a local high school, learn English and ultimately make a life for himself here in America. But despite having his parents and other relatives in the area, he found it difficult to make the transition to an American high school. His parents and the other adults he knew were too busy with their jobs, their own lives, to help him. After a period of his struggling and failing to adjust to school, Ivan's stepfather, who had served in the American Army in World War II, demanded that Ivan either join the Army or move out and be on his own. Ivan chose the latter.

Thus at age 17, unable to make a go of it on his own, Ivan found himself homeless in New York. He took various odd jobs and slept wherever he could, usually on the flat roofs of apartment buildings. (Rooftops are warmer and safer than street-level options.) Not surprisingly, under these abysmal living conditions, his life spiraled out of control. He was arrested numerous times, began to have mental issues and suffered from debilitating migraines. Ultimately, after an arrest for criminal trespass, he was committed to a mental institution for three months. Following that, he was sentenced, and he served 90 days in jail. Not surprisingly, these measures were in no way helpful.

However, as luck would have it, Ivan's cousin Patrick, a student at the University of Vermont, decided to help him. After looking into possible treatment options in the Burlington area, Patrick learned about the Howard Center, an organization that offers supportive services to individuals with mental health challenges who need help with counseling, medical services, employment and life management skills. After being accepted by the Howard Center as a patient, Ivan moved here and was finally able to get his life back on track.

Ivan had been to Burlington on a brief visit previously, right after arriving in this country, and he loved it. It was summer, the weather was cooperating, and it felt like a warm, safe place, somewhat reminiscent of home in Ecuador. This was in 1974, back when cars still drove up and down Church Street

Shutterstock

Quito, with one of Ecuador's active volcanoes only 30 miles away.

Typical Equadorian farming landscape, showing the extensive use of greenhouses.

and the Burlington Waterfront was a best-avoided industrial wasteland. Much has changed in Vermont and Burlington over the last 45 years, but Ivan has maintained his relationship with the Howard Center. He arrived in Burlington in dire straits, but today he is healthy, happy and employed as a cook for the Westview House, a day center on South Willard Street run by the Howard Center.

He didn't arrive here knowing how cook—far from it. Over the years he has worked all manner of jobs: gardening, raking, mowing, working for moving companies, stacking wood, bussing tables, shoveling snow and repairing furniture. But it was a job at the Radisson Hotel, serving food to the employees, and following that, preparing deli food at Price Chopper, that led him into cooking. He has gone from being a complete klutz in the kitchen to preparing Ecuadorian specialties.

Ivan is unmarried and lives with a roommate who is from Puerto Rico. When the two of them can't sort out their Spanish dialect differences, they fall back on English. As is typical for two speakers with two languages in common, they employ a mixture of English and Spanish. Why not use the combined expressive power of both languages?

Fruit stand in Otavalo, Ecuador, 2018.

Ivan preparing lunch at the Westview House, Burlington, 2018.

Ivan is 64 now, and a grandfather. His 26-year-old son Felix and his wife are the proud parents of a baby boy. When Ivan retires, in two or three years, he plans to return to Ecuador and settle near family there. He's heard there isn't much in the way of good pizza restaurants in Ecuador, and being the capable cook he is, he is thinking of opening "Ivan's Pizza" in Quito.

In the 47 years since he left Ecuador, Ivan has never paid a visit to the country of his birth. His childhood home will probably be unrecognizable to him, because Quito has grown in the meantime from the "small" city of 900,000 that he remembers to a city of over two million.

Katie Figura

‖‖‖

SUHAD MURAD

IRAQ

Suhad's story in her own words begins as follows:

We originally from Iraq. We lived all our lives in Iraq. We never planned to come here or anywhere. That's happened sudden, it's not happened like we planned to leave Iraq. After 2003 the situation got worse, worse and worse. Year by year it got worse. The neighborhood where we lived in Baghdad, it's too dangerous, people killed every day, friends, neighbors. They had a list of people to kill. Every day you don't know who is going to be killed. Then they say we are on the list. So we left, the whole family left. We left everything—house, business, everything—and escaped to Jordan.

In Iraq, Suhad, her husband Zaki Areef and their two children enjoyed a prosperous life. They lived in an upscale neighborhood in Baghdad. Zaki and his two brothers worked in the family market, a thriving grocery store about the size of Burlington's City Market, owned by their father.

In March 2003, the United States and coalition forces invaded Iraq, quickly overwhelming the Iraqi military. Saddam Hussein's government collapsed, and Saddam himself was captured in December and subsequently executed. An unintended consequence of the overthrow of Saddam was the brutal retaliation of Iraq's Shia population—they make up about 75% of the country—against the minority Sunni sect. In retrospect, since Saddam was Sunni, along with most members of his government, and given the historical animosity between these two major sects of Islam, this reaction is not surprising. With the removal of Saddam's government, the stage was set for the long-oppressed Shia majority to fill the power vacuum and to settle old scores. Shia militia quickly gained control of the country and mounted a formidable resistance, known as the Shia Insurgency, to the U.S.-led occupation forces. Today, 15 years later, to the extent that Iraq has a functioning government, it is a Shia government.

Suhad and her extended family are Sunnis, and though they were not combatants in the war, she and her family, as prominent, successful Sunnis, found themselves in mortal danger after the overthrow of Saddam.

As Suhad describes in the first paragraph, after the invasion their security situation gradually deteriorated. Finally, one day in 2005, based on a tip that they were on a "kill list," they fled to neighboring Jordan. At the time, Jordan was accepting very few Iraqi refugees, and while they knew that driving to Jordan was possible (it's about 500 miles from Baghdad to Amman, Jordan's capital), they believed they would not be allowed to cross the border. So they elected to fly, buying round-trip tickets to allay suspicion that they were fleeing the country. This meant they could take very little in the way of personal effects with them.

Katie Figura

Suhad and her husband, Zaki, 2018.

Aerial view of a typical Baghdad neighborhood.

As it turned out, some of the family were allowed into Jordan, but Suhad, her husband Zaki and their two children were denied entry. Fortunately, they were able to continue to Syria. After a miserable six months in Syria, living in limbo with no opportunity to make a living—they had to live off savings and help from family members to survive—they were allowed to move to Jordan. In the meantime, Zaki's father had set up a grocery store in Amman, providing a livelihood for the family.

Meanwhile, back in Baghdad, the family business was kept running by loyal employees. However, two months after Suhad and her family left the country, the dreaded visit from the Shia "police" arrived at the store. Arriving in officially marked cars, the militants interrogated the workers, asking for their names to determine who was Shia and who was Sunni. The Shia employees were told to leave. The Sunni employees were executed on the spot and the store was burned, a total loss. Four of Zaki's relatives were among those murdered.

After two years in Jordan, in 2007, they were informed that they could emigrate to the United States, and in June of 2008 they arrived in

all photos Katie Figura

Suhad's mother, recently arrived from Iraq, 2018.

Green beans and eggplant from Nada Market.

Ahmed, Suhad's brother-in-law, in the family's Nada Market, April 2019.

Burlington. They lived first in Winooski, then in Colchester, and are now happily settled in Essex Junction. Once again, the family patriarch has been able to establish a grocery store, the very popular Nada (Nadia) Market on Main Street in Winooski. Serving an international selection of meat, fruit and vegetables, as well as teas, coffees and desserts, Nada is a Winooski mainstay for immigrants and longtime locals alike.

108

Cruz Alberto "Beto" Sanchez-Perez

MEXICO

Alberto left Mexico because he is gay. His family and friends accepted him, but two serious beatings and Mexico's intensely homophobic atmosphere left no doubt that life as an openly gay man in Mexico would be a life of uncertainty and danger. Officially, Mexico is increasingly accepting of the LGBTQ community—Mexico was the first Latin American country to legalize same-sex marriage—but the rate of violent crimes against gay individuals remains high. Thus, he decided to try to make a go of it in this country. His younger brother was already working on a farm in Vermont, and between the two of them they had enough money to pay for Alberto to be smuggled across the border. After making the necessary arrangements, Alberto flew to Monterrey, a city in northern Mexico, where he met Paco, the man who would guide him across the border into Texas.

Paco is a coyote, one who helps Latin Americans without visas cross the border into the United States—for a hefty fee. After being transported from Monterrey to a remote location closer to the border, Paco, Alberto and Paco's 10 other clients rested while they waited until night. In the darkness, they set out on foot, reaching the border—the Rio Grande—after walking all night. Before crossing the river, Paco gave the men plastic bags to keep their clothes dry; those who couldn't swim were given inner tubes to hang

109

on to. The water was cold but the current slack, and Alberto swam across the narrow river easily. After resting and drying off, they continued north across the dry, uninhabited landscape, from time to time encountering high fences which they climbed over without difficulty. The occasional border patrols were spotted in time for them to avoid detection by crouching down in low spots in the terrain. Eventually they came to a major highway, and at this point, after three days on the move—walking at night and resting during the day—Paco announced that he had completed his role in their journey and would be handing them over to others who would carry out the final stage. He explained to Alberto what to expect:

> Tomorrow you are going to be picked up by a truck that is used for animal transport. What they are going to do is toss you in there like animals. You don't want to be first, but you don't want to be last and end up on top either, because if the truck is chased, they are going to drive really fast—on a bumpy gravel road—and there's a good chance you will be thrown off. So lie on your side and try to avoid having others on top of you.

Chad Zuber, Shutterstock

At the border wall, Mexican families living in Tijuana talk with family members living in the U.S.

Caleb Kenna

Vermont migrant workers at the end of their work day.

As promised, the next day a truck appeared, and after paying Paco his fee—Alberto and the others each paid him 1500 dollars—they were loaded into the vehicle as Paco had described. After an uneventful ride, they arrived in a small town farther north and were dropped off at what seemed to be an abandoned warehouse, but once inside, they were met by armed guards. The guards escorted Alberto and his fellow travelers, one by one, to the boss of the smuggling operation to make their final payment of 5,000 dollars. Some paid in cash; others made calls to initiate wire transfers. It goes without saying that no one was free to go until payment was made. From here, using safe houses and an underground transportation network, Alberto and the other men—now illegal immigrants—continued to their various destinations in the United States.

The events described above took place almost four years ago. Today, at age 27, Alberto is employed at a large dairy farm in northern Vermont. Known for his cheerful demeanor regardless of the weather or the task at hand, he arrives at the heifer barn before dawn, ready to work. His co-worker, Sue, describes Alberto's work day:

Alberto starts work at 5 a.m. and does six days a week with one day off. His duties in the calf facility at the farm include feeding the newborn calves milk, cleaning their pens, putting out hay and grain and putting straw down on heifer packs. Then he and his brother clean the big heifer barns, alternating which ones each day. Alberto found another job he loved which was feeding chickens and collecting eggs for one of the owners. His day usually ends around 5 p.m. My favorite thing about him is his attitude toward detail and doing things right—such a happy person!

On his day off Alberto relaxes, runs errands, does some cooking for the coming week and hangs out with friends. On hot summer days, he is likely to ride his bike a few miles to the local swimming hole. Together with three other migrant workers. In summary, it seems Alberto made a good choice in coming to America: he has made many friends here, both Mexican and American, both gay and straight, and he is a valued employee in an important sector of our local economy.

Unfortunately, the scenario described above was upended on December 31, 2018. At his court hearing in Middlebury for a DUI charge in early December, Alberto was arrested by Immigration and Customs Enforcement (ICE) agents inside the courthouse, taken into custody and slated for deportation.

Since he was an undocumented Mexican farm worker, Alberto was immediately transported to federal prison, in New Hampshire, to await almost certain deportation. As a vulnerable individual, he feared for his safety in prison; fortunately he was able reduce his time spent with the general prison population by having his meals brought to him in his cell. His brother, Luis, and his co-worker, Sue, were extremely supportive throughout his time in prison. They were able to stay in touch by phone and to send him money to supplement the meager prison rations, and to rent movies. Finally, after almost three months of tense waiting, including the disappointment of two cancelled court dates, Alberto was granted his hearing. Two factors would greatly influence the outcome. First, months prior to his arrest for DUI—an arrest that may or may not have been justified—Alberto and his lawyer had applied for asylum based on the danger implicit in his returning to Mexico. Secondly, Alberto's history of abuse and exploitation in Mexico had been carefully documented by his sister and made available this material was presented to the court. Alberto gives us an idea of his early life:

It is not easy for me to talk about my past and all the unfortunate things I have experienced since I am seven or eight. Wherever I went I was

Alberto taking part in a Milk with Dignity March, Burlington, 2018.

mistreated because I am gay, so much discrimination, bullying. Because I am gay, people saw me like I am not worthy...all the macho men humiliating me...so difficult to see how they look at you, just because you are gay. Why me? I am a good person, humble, poor. I wanted a childhood where I could play, go to school, without being mocked. I wanted friends who didn't demand something in return. I wanted to be a normal child, with people that would listen to me, understand and help me. I only thought about turning 18 so I could leave home, but that was the hardest, because the city treated me the worst.

Alberto's time in prison had a happy ending: he was granted indefinite asylum status and he is now back at his old job. It bears mentioning that Alberto received huge support from Burlington's Migrant Justice organization and the community at large. Over a thousand people petitioned on his behalf; others, including Vermont's congressional delegation, wrote letters of support.

IIIII

PEMBA SHERPA

NEPAL

On his historic first ascent of Mount Everest in 1953, Edmund Hillary was so impressed with his hard-working, tough and always-cheerful Sherpa companions that he vowed to do something to improve their quality of life. In 1961, making good on his promise, Hillary was able to oversee the construction of the Everest Region's first school, in the village of Khumjung, located at 13,000 feet, about five days' walk from Everest Base Camp. A few years later, Hillary founded the area's first hospital in Khunde, the adjoining village to the west. Both villages are shown in the photo on the next page. Today, almost 50 years later, the school and the hospital are thriving and are key components of the Sherpa community.

Pemba Sherpa was born in Khumjung village and grew up there. His family led a simple farming life, caring for the family's sheep, cows and other animals, working in their fields, finding and carrying firewood and collecting mushrooms for food. Pemba attended the school that Hillary founded, graduating in 1993. He then moved to the capital city, Kathmandu, and after college studies, including learning Japanese, he worked on various climbing and trekking expeditions. He married Ming Sherpa in 1997, and five years later they moved to Burlington where he, his wife and their twin daughters, Chetan and Chewang, now live.

Jared Gange

The villages of Khumjung (right) and Khunde, with Mount Everest in the center distance and iconic Ama Dablam on the right.

Growing up in Khumjung, Pemba's family, and most of the villagers, were subsistence farmers. The setting is staggeringly beautiful, and the air and water pure and clear, but life here is far from easy and not without attendant health issues. The main crops are potatoes, buckwheat, radishes, carrots, cauliflower, beans, scallions, mustard greens and spinach. Most families have yaks, cows and dzo, the yak–cow crossbreed. In years past, Pemba's grandparents and other relatives had a lot of sheep, but nowadays only one family has sheep, and just a few. The animals supply them with wool, milk, transportation and manure for fertilizer. Rice, tea and lentils are all-important in the Nepalese diet, but they must be transported up from the lowlands—carried on the backs of porters—because they can't be cultivated in the high, cold climate of the Everest Region. Homemade butter and cheese supplement their diet, and tea is the main drink. However, tea as prepared Sherpa-style, with butter—sometimes rancid, as there is no refrigeration—and salt, wouldn't be recognized as tea by most outsiders. For us westerners, it's more like a strange soup.

As kids, in the spring and summer, and especially on rainy days, Pemba and his friends would go into nearby woods to collect mushrooms. They

116

preferred to go in groups because of the possibility of an encounter with wild dogs or the occasional bear. During the harsh winter months, because of the greater effort required to maintain a remotely satisfactory existence, families need all the help they can get. As a result, kids are let out of school to help with chores. Of necessity, Pemba and the other village boys made weekly treks to get firewood, there being no firewood nearby. This involved trekking three hours, finding and cutting dry wood, eating a quick lunch and hurrying back with their loads to reach home before dark. As is common in these mountain regions, yak dung is collected, dried and used to supplement precious firewood. Ventilation in the simple Sherpa homes is usually inadequate, and given the already smoky dung fires, serious lung and eye ailments are unfortunately very common, especially among women. Pemba's mother, who never smoked, died of lung cancer at the age of 55. Pemba himself missed a year of school because of a bout of tuberculosis.

Pemba has inherited the family home and land. He rents out the house, but the land is no longer farmed. This is a common scenario, as many of the current generation of Sherpas have left the area or live there only part time. Some have emigrated to India, Europe, or the U.S., seeking a more financially secure and less demanding way of life. And many have simply found work in other areas of Nepal, especially Kathmandu. But some who

Leo Murray

Expedition porter carrying a typical load, on his way to Mount Everest.

have stayed have achieved significant financial success, even fame, through mountaineering expeditions. Several Sherpas have climbed Everest over a dozen times. The record, as of 2018, is 22 ascents, held by 48-year-old Kami Rita Sherpa. And while there are some who still follow the old way of life—pre-1960 or so—the area has been transformed economically and socially. It is an irony that Hillary's well-meaning efforts—a hospital, many schools and the area's two airstrips—have in no small way contributed to the demise of the traditional way of life in the Everest Region. Perhaps there is solace in the fact that since change is unavoidable, his projects have at least been a positive factor.

At 11,300 feet, Namche Bazaar is the Sherpa capital. Of the various villages clinging to the mountainsides in the Everest Region, it is the only one that could be called a town. As such, it is the staging point for climbing and trekking expeditions. The easiest way to reach Namche Bazaar is by a short flight from Kathmandu to the Lukla airstrip (9,400 feet), one of the most dangerous airports in the world. From there one walks about a day and a half to Namche, at 11,300 feet. Pemba's home village, Khumjung, is at 13,000 feet, another 2 hours' climb above Namche. The

Jared Gange

Boudhanath, one of the largest and oldest Buddhist stupas in the world. Kathmandu, Nepal.

Pemba Sherpa

Burlington High School graduation, 2017. Pemba's wife Ming and their twin daughters Chetan and Chewang.

entire area is roadless. Throughout the region food, cooking fuel and most other supplies—stoves, toilets, lumber and kerosene, to name a few—are transported by porters, with some loads as heavy as 200 pounds.

The Sherpa language is related to Tibetan, as the Sherpas' ancestors originated in Tibet, having wandered south over the Himalayan Range into Nepal about 500 years ago. To this day, yak caravans ply the ancient trade route from Namche Bazaar, over the 19,000-foot Nangpa La Pass, into Chinese-controlled Tibet. The yaks return from Tibet with inexpensive Chinese clothes and household goods.

After working for years as a cook, Pemba now works with his wife in their cleaning business. He visits Nepal regularly, every couple of years. He stays with relatives in Kathmandu or in Khumjung, usually visiting for a month or two. He is unsure what to do with his house and land in Khumjung. He could use the house as a summer place but has no desire to live there year-round. One of his daughters would like to live in Nepal for a year after high school, but Pemba insists she finish college first.

All in all, Pemba and his family are happy here in the U.S. and Vermont. Both he and his wife are employed; they own their own home and car. During the warmer months, Pemba enjoys riding his Suzuki motorcycle. He and Ming have many friends, and the girls are completely assimilated and do very well in school. Slowly, Burlington's small Sherpa community is growing.

PALESTINE

There is today no territory officially known as Palestine. But for hundreds of years, up to the mid-20th century, maps of the lands at the eastern end of the Mediterranean showed an area labeled Palestine. Most of the territory once known as Palestine is now known as Israel, and current maps no longer show Palestine. However, there are over 12 million Palestinians, about half of whom do not live in Israel, have never been to Israel and cannot easily visit Israel—the former Palestine, the home of their parents, their grandparents and their ancestors.

Some may find the above statements offensive, an oversimplification, even untrue. Indeed, 137 member countries of the United Nations do recognize Palestine as a sovereign state within the boundaries of Israel. But it is a state in name only, a state in theory. It is a state with no accepted boundaries, a state with a mockery of self-governance, with no legal system, no monetary system or currency, a state of hope in a place of hopelessness. Hence Palestine, as a country, is recognized by neither the United States nor the United Nations.

The fundamental fact about this area of the Middle East is that it is sacred to three major religions: Christianity, Islam and Judaism. Sites of enormous religious importance—to one or more of these faiths—are scattered throughout the region. Over the centuries Palestine has been controlled by various groups—Romans, Canaanites, Phoenicians, Jews and Philistines—to name a few. But from the 12th century onward, the area was under the control of one Muslim state or another, concluding with the Ottoman Empire. After World War I (1914–1918), the Ottoman Empire was dissolved and the British assumed control of Palestine as a spoil of war. In 1922, the League of Nations, precursor to the United Nations, formalized British administration of Palestine, and Britain's subsequent stewardship—the Mandate for Palestine, or British Mandate, as it was known—prevailed until 1948.

In 1922, the population of Palestine was overwhelmingly Muslim—around 80%—with Jews and Christians accounting for about 10% each, but the area's demographics were undergoing rapid change. Greatly influenced by the tenets of the Zionist Movement, a worldwide Jewish immigration to Palestine was under way. The Zionist Movement persuasively advanced the notion that the Jews of the world, the Jewish diaspora, deserved, and

Palestinian children leaving their recently destroyed, then provisionally rebuilt, school in the West Bank.

should have, a country of their own, a place to settle and live their lives in safety, free from persecution and discrimination. The Zionists' logical but bold choice for settlement was Palestine, which, according to the Zionist slogan at the time, was deemed "A land with no people, for a people with no land." This incredible claim ignored the fact that Palestine was then home to about 700,000 Arab Palestinians. Britain pledged support for the creation of a Jewish home within Palestine, while also pledging to respect the rights of the indigenous Arab (Palestinian) population.

As the 20th century progressed, more and more Jewish settlers established themselves in Palestine, taking over Arab lands by both legal and illegal means. The Palestinian population's increasing unease with the steady influx of settlers, combined with newcomers' determination to establish a Jewish state, eroded the generally peaceful coexistence that had prevailed between the Jewish and Arab communities.

In the mid- and late 1930s, the British responded to Arab demands to curtail Jewish immigration and land acquisition, but this led to violent pushback from Jewish militants. It is from this increasingly violent atmosphere, involving deadly attacks on both sides, that we can trace the beginnings of what has become a refugee problem of enormous scale. At present, in 2019, there are approximately 6 million Palestinian refugees. They are scattered throughout the world but the majority live in refugee camps in Jordan, Syria, Lebanon and Israel itself. (The current war in Syria has generated some 11 million refugees, many of whom are presumably Palestinians.)

In 1947, following the Britain's decision to terminate its administration of Palestine, the United Nations put forth a suggested division of Palestinian territory—known as the Partition Plan—which allocated approximately equal portions of territory to the Jewish and Arab populations. While accepted by the Jewish community—at least as a starting point—Palestinians rejected the plan out of hand as overly generous to the Jewish side, considering its considerably smaller population. As the British departure date (May 15, 1948) approached, Jewish militia stepped up attacks on Palestinian villages and urban areas, and in March of 1948, Jewish leadership set in motion so-called Plan D. Essentially an ethnic cleansing directive, and consistent with the Zionist aim of achieving an exclusively Jewish presence in Palestine, Plan D provided military units with lists of Palestinian villages to bomb and demolish: homes and property were to be burned and the remaining rubble

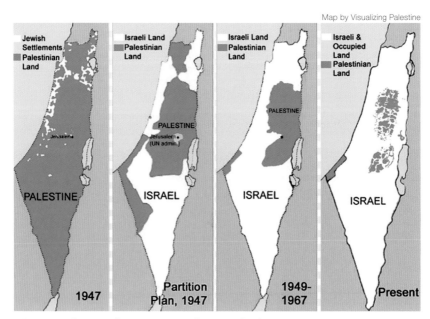

Map by Visualizing Palestine

Map series showing the progressive reduction of Palestinian territory.

mined, thus preventing inhabitants from returning. Over the following six months the better-armed and better-funded Jewish forces carried out Plan D: over 500 Palestinian villages were destroyed. On May 15, 1948, the official departure date of the British, the Jewish community declared itself to be the sovereign State of Israel. Known to Palestinians as "al-Naqba," the Catastrophe, May 15 is Israel's Independence Day.

Following May 15, Israel was attacked by its Arab neighbors Jordan, Egypt, Syria and Iraq, and the existing civil war expanded to a full-blown regional war known as the Arab–Israeli War of 1948. Again Israel prevailed, thanks in no small part to significant military support from European allies. At the end of the war, in July of 1949, Israel retained the land allocated to it by the UN Partition Plan, as well as 60% of the UN-designated Palestinian territory (see map). It is estimated that as a result of this war, over 700,000 Palestinians either fled or were expelled from their homes. For 70 years—ever since the war ended—Israel has prevented these individuals, and their children, and their childrens' children from returning to their home territory, the land of their ancestors.

However, the subjugation and oppression of Palestinians goes well beyond the existence of refugees and Israel's denial of their "right of return" to their homes. For example, in the West Bank, Palestinians lead an extremely constrained existence. (Seized in the 1967 Six-Day War, the West Bank comprises one quarter of the total territory controlled by Israel.) Aspects of life for Palestinians include humiliation and harassment at heavily armed checkpoints, prison detention without charge, devastating collective punishment, sniper killings of children, harsh sentences for minor infractions, steady appropriation of Palestinian land, limited access to one's own land and random, unpredictable treatment in interactions with the Israeli army, the IDF (Israeli Defense Forces).

To be sure, Israel has reason to distrust and fear Palestinians. Rockets are occasionally launched at Israeli targets, soldiers are shot or stabbed, suicide bombers have killed hundreds and rock throwing at soldiers is commonplace. As self-destructive as these actions are, they are understandable when one has nothing left to lose, but their glorification by Palestinians undermines the Palestinian cause. Even so, in the unending chain of revenge, these actions pale compared to the orders-of-magnitude-greater retaliation consistently meted out by Israel.

Wherever one stands on the areas of disagreement between the Israelis and the Palestinians, it is an inescapable fact that approximately half of Israel's resident population—the Palestinians—is not accorded the same status as the Jewish population. Furthermore, this state of affairs, which varies from moderate to the most extreme deprivation, is completely under the control of, and is perpetuated by, the State of Israel. Thus, in the view of many informed observers, including many Israelis, Israel is functionally an apartheid state.

The following statement, attributed to David Ben-Gurion (1886–1973), founder and first prime minister of Israel, speaks to the intractable nature of the Israeli–Palestinian conflict:

> If I were an Arab leader, I would never sign an agreement with Israel. It is normal; we have taken their country. It is true God promised it to us, but how could that interest them? Our God is not theirs. There has been anti-Semitism, the Nazis, Hitler, Auschwitz, but was that their fault? They see but one thing: we have come and we have stolen their country. Why would they accept that?

The Palestinians didn't accept it then and they don't accept it now. Today, 70 years later, they and their descendants are at best second-class citizens in a country that was once theirs. To illustrate how difficult life is for Palestinians living in the West Bank—and how little known this is—consider the

Laurie Gagne/Meta Peace Team

Israeli settlers destroying an irrigation pipe belonging to Palestinian farmers, Bardela, West Bank, 2018.

A Palestinian woman pleads her case with Israeli soldiers at a checkpoint in the Arab city of Hebron, in the West Bank, territory captured by Israel in 1967.

following from Uri Savir, Israel's chief negotiator (1993–1996) for the Oslo Accords, a set of agreements addressing the Israeli–Palestinian situation:

> What I discovered was that a West Bank Palestinian could not work, build, study, purchase land, grow produce, start a business, take a walk at night, visit his family in Gaza, enter Israel or travel abroad without a permit from us and that we had imprisoned about one third of the entire Palestinian population.

The Oslo Accords were ground-breaking peace talks of great promise that unfortuneatly, over time, failed to provide a resolution to the conflict. Splitting Israel into a Jewish state and a Palestinian state has its appeal, but an equal division of territory is unacceptable to the Israeli government, particularly given the systematic, ongoing takeover of Palestinian land by Jewish settlers. The logical, albeit utopian solution of one inclusive nation, based on equal rights for all, would render impossible a Jewish state, even a majority Jewish state, as Israel's Palestinians are on track to outnumber Israel's Jewish population within a few years. Unfortunately, if history is any indication, peaceful coexistence in either of the above scenarios would require a seismic shift in attitude on both sides.

126

‖‖‖

WAFIC FAOUR

PALESTINE

Wafic was born in a refugee camp in Lebanon. Twelve years earlier, in 1948, his parents, then in their late teens, had been forced to flee their homes in Palestine to safety in nearby Lebanon. They would live out their lives in Lebanon, never allowed to return to their home village in Palestine, even for a visit.

Wafic's parents were part of one of the largest forced migrations in modern history. According to the renowned Israeli historian Ilan Pappe, "Around a million people were expelled from their homes at gunpoint, civilians were massacred, and hundreds of Palestinians villages were destroyed. Denied for almost six decades, had it happened today it could only have been called ethnic cleansing." Terrorist tactics employed by the Jewish militia, involving the carefully planned, systematic obliteration of Palestinian villages, were a key component of the strategy to create an exclusively Jewish state in Palestine. In the resulting chaos, even those who were spared violence abandoned their homes in panic, thus swelling the numbers of Palestinians fleeing their homes and their country, a country known henceforth as Israel.

A large portion of this flood of refugees settled in Lebanon. Wafic, his parents and siblings lived near the coastal city of Tyre, in Rashedia Camp, only 40 miles from their ancestral home of Sha'ab in Palestine. Living

The Palestinian village of Sha'ab in northern Israel, ancestral home of Wafic's family.

conditions were abysmal. *The poverty was unbelievable,* according to Wafic. Their entire family of 10 was crammed into two tiny rooms totaling 100 square feet; 100 square feet is the size of a small bedroom.

Wafic describes their daily routine:

> Most of the time when we sleep, we sleep on mattresses on the floor and in the morning you put the mattresses together. When we stack the mattresses on top of each other, there will be a space to sit down. This is what happens every morning. It will become a floor for breakfast and we eat on the (cement) floor.

With eight children in such a small space, their living conditions were beyond crowded, but as Wafic recalls:

> I had a great, great time growing up with a big family. I got a lot of support, we give and take a lot of support from each other. To this day, I have a very strong relationship with my brothers and sisters.

The majority of Palestinian refugees in Lebanon are not granted the rights enjoyed by Lebanese citizens and remain stateless. While refugees, Wafic's parents among them, are able to work, run businesses and live outside of the camps, they are not allowed to own property, or their businesses, under Lebanese law. This can be circumvented through proxy ownership, via a spouse or other relative by marriage who is Lebanese, thus providing a path for some to achieve a measure of economic well-being.

Partly as a result of initiatives by the UN, and partly due to their high regard for education, Palestinians as a group—throughout their diaspora—are well educated. As Wafic puts it: *As impoverished refugees, education is the only commodity you have.* When Wafic was growing up, free primary and secondary schooling was available to him, and at age 17 with assistance from the American Friends of the Middle East, he applied to, and was accepted by, several American colleges. His father's business was doing well enough to cover his expenses, and in September 1978, Wafic left Lebanon and enrolled at Northeastern University in Boston. He has lived in New England ever since, moving to Vermont in 1991.

Although Wafic had to drop out of college after three years—his family could no longer afford the tuition—his years at Northeastern were profoundly formative, even life-defining. When he first arrived in Boston, fresh from refugee camp life, Wafic came in contact with students from Iran who were vigorously protesting their country's monarch and his repressive regime. Inspired by their example, and the work of the university's organization of Arab students, Wafic became an activist, too. After leaving Northeastern, he

Catay, Shutterstock

Sabra and Shatila refugee camp in Beirut, Lebanon, February 2018.

worked for local nonprofits that advocated for the Palestinian cause, and to support himself, he worked a variety of jobs: bussing tables, washing dishes and as a security guard. As money and time allowed, he attended courses at Boston University and the University of Massachusetts Boston.

Meanwhile, events back in Lebanon only served to heighten his determination to bring attention to the plight of Palestinians. In June 1982, responding to attacks and other militant Palestinian activity in the Lebanon–Israel border region, Israel's army, the IDF—Israeli Defense Forces—invaded southern Lebanon, triggering war and bringing long-term destabilization to Lebanon. The war officially ended in 1995, but in Lebanon, destruction and loss of life continued for years, leaving the country and its capital Beirut devastated. On the personal side, Wafic's parents' home was bombed and destroyed, erasing years of hard work.

Wafic describes how his parents coped:

They started from scratch again. They got help from my sister working in Saudi Arabia. Father started again with selling recycled oil. He also bought oil from the Arab Emirates wholesale, then canned it and sold it onward. Always you dust yourself off, you start again.

In 1991, when his older sister Wafica and her husband Yasin left Saudi Arabia after working for Aramco, an Arabian–American oil company, they moved to Vermont and bought a business in Colchester. They asked Wafic to move here and work with them. This he did, and he has worked in the family business to this day.

Wafic and his wife Helene have two children: Zane, 17, and Kamli, 20. Kamli attends Middlebury College and is a pre-med major, with a minor in Arabic studies. She is becoming fluent in Arabic and shares her father's passion for the Palestinian cause.

Wafic has been able to return to Lebanon many times to visit relatives, many of whom still live a refugee existence, but he has never seen his parents' village and has never been to Israel. Adding to the frustration is the fact that Sha'ab is only 25 miles directly south of the Lebanese border, about 50 miles from where Wafic grew up, near Tyre. While it is possible to drive from Tyre to Sha'ab, the shortest legal route is a roundabout 8-hour, 250-mile jaunt that leads into Syria, then south into Jordan, and from there west into Israel, before turning north to Sha'ab, completing the circular route. It is as if, when driving from Burlington to Rutland, your best route were via Boston, with two international border crossings thrown in.

In recent years, Wafic has been working with the Vermont Coalition for Ethnic Studies and Social Equity in Schools, a multicultural and multigenerational group made up of individuals from various racial and ethnic groups, including anti-poverty and disability rights advocates and LGBTQIA advocates. The goal of the Coalition is to move our society toward a more balanced educational approach in our schools, an approach that more equitably reflects the experiences and histories of traditionally disenfranchised groups.

He is also active in Vermonters for Justice in Palestine, an organization committed to the principles of self-determination for the Palestinian people, the right of return for Palestinian refugees and full civil and political rights for all Palestinians, in order to promote the equality and safety of both Palestinians and Israelis.

When asked what Palestinians could do differently in the effort to normalize relations between Israel and the Palestinians, Wafic responds:

> This a wrong point: You are making both sides equal. We are not equal, so it's not like each side doing something to break it (the impasse). We are on the receiving end. We are the unarmed resistance, doing things like BDS (the Boycott, Divestment and Sanctions) movement. But even BDS might become illegal—in the United States!

To the question of what Palestinians can do, given the current state of affairs, he responds:

> It's not what we will do. There is facts on the ground. The demographic has changed, which is the number of the Palestinians between the water and the water—from the Jordan River to the Mediterranean Sea—they are becoming the majority. If Israel wants to include the West Bank in a single state, and give the same rights to all of its citizens, including "one man, one vote" it will have to deal with the fact of a Palestinian majority.

Wafic gives a summary of the Palestinian perspective:

> The story of the Holocaust is brought up every time we talk about Israel: but what do I have to do with it? The Holocaust was carried out by white Christians. Why should I pay for it? Why my father pay for it? Why a Jewish person born in Vermont can go and have a passport over there and passport over here and my mother and my father when they die are not allowed to be buried next to their parents. We are not equal. Israel dictates what's happening, by force.

‖‖‖

VALERY KAGAN

RUSSIA

When Valery Kagan was five years old, World War II had been underway for two years, and a massive German army was rapidly taking control of Ukraine, the homeland of Val's family. With its fertile soil and favorable climate, Ukraine was known as the Breadbasket of Europe, and capturing it was a key element of the Third Reich's strategy. Fearing brutal treatment at the hands of the Germans, and probably death, millions of Ukrainians fled the advancing armies. Val and his family, being Jewish, were especially vulnerable.

To deny the Germans valuable infrastructure—Europe's largest hydro power plant was in Ukraine—Russia had adopted a policy of demolishing bridges, factories and power plants before the Germans could capture them. Val's father, a chemistry professor, had been assigned to one of the "demolition units," and at one point in 1941, completely by chance, he found himself in their now nearly abandoned home city of Kharkov.

On impulse he decided to look in on their apartment, and to his shock and horror, he found Val, his 15-year-old daughter and his mother-in-law still living there. His wife, hospitalized with complications after surgery, had been unable to organize their escape. He immediately took the children to their mother, removed her from the hospital on a stretcher and delivered

Val and Tanya in Novosibirsk, newly married.

them all to the last train transport out of Kharkov. His mother-in-law refused to leave the apartment and was subsequently killed by the Germans.

What followed was a bizarre three-month-long train journey, ultimately ending deep in the interior of Russia at the remote Siberian city of Novosibirsk. Their train—the cars were designed for cattle transport—was repeatedly bombed by German planes and frequently delayed by more urgent train traffic to and from the war's frontlines. During these attacks, the "passengers" would leave the train and hide, returning to the train when the all-clear signal was given. Unfortunately, in the confusion, this led to children, or parents, being left behind, wreaking havoc with families.

Miraculously, Val's mother recovered during the journey, and when they reached Novosibirsk, she was assigned to a hospital where she, a doctor, was needed to tend to the war wounded. When they arrived, they lived first in a train station, then as unwelcome guests (assigned by the authorities) in a local home and finally in an unused school building.

During the war years, life was far from normal, despite the fact that the actual fighting was far away. Schoolteachers treated their pupils like their own children, as most children had no fathers at home, having lost them to the war effort. Due to the extreme shortage of paper, students wrote their lessons in the narrow white space between the printed lines of discarded newspapers. Women were used as draft animals, because horses were needed at the front. To prevent their capture by the Germans, entire factories were hastily transported away from the war zone to Novosibirsk, where they were reassembled out in the open, operating in the rain and snow, until roofs could be built. Power lines to these rudimentary factories were simply laid on the ground, sometimes running for several kilometers. The disciple imposed on workers was unimaginably harsh: if you were 15 minutes late for work, you could be sent to prison, 30 minutes late and you could be shot.

With the war's end, in 1945, their circumstances improved and life gradually returned to normal. A brilliant student, Val graduated from high school with the highest honors. In the Russian education system this meant that Val could attend any university in Russia without taking entrance exams. His dream was to become a nuclear physicist. He applied to the prestigious University of Moscow, only to be told that, in his case, he would have to take entrance exams. Despite acing the exams, he, as a Jew, was denied acceptance.

Out for a winter stroll in Novosibirsk, Siberia.

Forced to abandon his dream of studying nuclear physics, he returned to Novosibirsk and studied electro-mechanical engineering at Novosibirsk Technical University. While at the university, he started a student jazz orchestra that is still active today, almost 60 years later. He continued to do well academically, finishing his undergraduate work and meeting and marrying Tanya, a fellow student. Like Val, Tanya went on to earn a PhD, hers in applied mathematics.

As a young adult, Val had last seen his father when he was five. Val saw him only one

135

other time, when he was 26. His father was badly wounded in the war, and after his long convalescence in Stalingrad, far from Novosibirsk, he married his Moldavian nurse. They later settled in Moldova, a part of the (former) Soviet Union between Ukraine and Romania.

Val completed his PhD in Electro Drive and Automation Control, and while working for his doctorate, he worked in various industrial settings, for plants producing large machine tools, injection molding machines, steel rolling mills and hydroelectric generators. After receiving his degree, he began a 25-year career as a professor at Novosibirsk Technical University, earning a second doctorate, Doctor of Science in Technical Cybernetics. He built up a department of research and development that by 1990 had a staff of 260. Val was renowned as a teacher, administrator and scientist, and through its research and development work, his institute generated 30% of the university's total budget. During vacations he and Tanya skied and climbed in some of the great mountain ranges of the world: the Pamir Range, the Caucasus and the Tien Shan mountains on Russia's border with China. These were happy and productive years for Val and his family.

Then came Perestroika. Originally intended as a modest restructuring of the Soviet political and economic systems, Perestroika ultimately led to the unraveling of the Soviet Union. By 1991, adverse effects were being

Hazelett Corporation

Val with his magnetic backup roll, used to stabilize belts running between cold water and molten copper, a temperature difference of 1,000 degrees centigrade.

felt, including the breakdown of the Soviet government's central planning and the funding of research. At this point, since their younger daughter Julie had already immigrated to the U.S., Val and Tanya decided to follow suit and join her, in Burlington, as it turned out. Times were not good here either—the country was in a deep recession—and finding a job commensurate with his skills and experience turned out to be impossible. He did odd jobs, including playing piano at a local bar. Eventually, an IBM engineer who realized Val's potential forwarded his resume to the Hazelett Corporation in Colchester.

Hazelett and Val were a great fit, as Hazelett designs and manufactures continuous casting equipment, an area similar to Val's background. After observing operations for a month, Val was able to suggest improvements in one of the production processes; his modifications are still in use. Following a minimally paid nine-month trial, during which Val made more improvements, Hazelett hired him as a full-time employee.

Today, at 82, Val has worked at Hazelett 27 years and is their chief scientist. He holds over 300 patents in Russia and 50 in the United States. He has written seven books and hundreds of articles. In 2014, he returned to Novosibirsk as an honored guest at his former institute, his first trip back in 20 years. Val's description of life in Russia today:

> From material point of view people live better, but ideologically worse. Very high level of anti-Western and anti-American propaganda in all media. They say America and West would like to destroy Russia, take Russian resources; oil, metals, [and] would like to make Russia a colony of the West. Therefore, Russia has to increase expenses for military, make bombs better than the West. The young, non-experienced people believe this. When I left Russia, it was empty supermarket, right now it is possible to buy everything. I told them that it is wrong to think that money comes from the sky in America. You have to work hard. If you work hard and make some good engineering thing, it is good life, and your invention will go directly to commercialization. In your private life you can do what you want—all freedoms.

138

Modou Ndione

SENEGAL

Modou grew up in the countryside, in a small village in the West African nation of Senegal. His family's home was a large thatched hut with a dirt floor, big enough to accommodate his parents and his five siblings. Their sleeping area had a room for his mom and dad, a room for the boys and a room for the girls. They had two bathrooms, one inside the hut and one outside. The outside bathroom was for the kids to use. The kitchen was in a separate hut, just a few steps away, and was made of mud, rather than thatch, for fire safety. Their homemade beds were made with branches from the acacia tree, and for mattresses they used huge bags—originally used to hold 300 pounds of rice—stuffed with leaves.

Modou's family was self-sufficient, supplying most of their food from their cows, goats, lambs and chickens and by growing peanuts, maize and millet. Some of the crop they kept for their own use; the rest they sold. Any meat had to be eaten within two days, as they had no refrigeration. The foundation of their diet was millet, a highly nutritious grain with a slightly nutty flavor. When ground to a fine powder, it is used to make couscous, the food staple of millions of people throughout North Africa and the Middle East. Peanuts were ground and combined with milk to make a sauce for the couscous.

Modou describes the morning routine:

My mom makes coffee every morning. She roasts and grinds the beans every day. Early in the morning when you hear that, you wake up. I would give her a hand with the grinding. Everybody in my family drinks coffee and eats the leftover couscous from the night before for breakfast.

Senegal is located on the very western edge of North Africa. It is similar to New England in area and population, but the capital, Dakar, is huge, with a population of about 2.5 million. Senegal is a land of many languages—the main ones are Wolof, Fula and Serer—but French remains the official language, a legacy of the French colonial period that lasted from 1677 to independence in 1960.

Senegal's tropical climate is characterized by distinct wet and dry seasons. Farming is the primary focus in the rainy season. The dry season, since the crops require less attention then, is the time for children to attend school.

Modou thinks back on his childhood days:

I always took pleasure in working the fields and taking care of the cattle. Going to the fields meant escaping into nature, and that was a space of freedom. When I was striding along the paths to the fields, I would feel

Modou Ndione

Modou and his family sharing a meal.

an immense joy invading me. I could listen to the songs of the birds and the insects and try to imitate them. I could listen to the murmur of the bushes. These were moments of spiritual delight. I have always carried these memories that soften the soul and open up the spirit to the mysteries of nature.

Modou's parents strongly encouraged their kids to get an education beyond primary school. For Modou and his siblings, this meant leaving their village and spending the school terms in the towns that had schools beyond the primary level. Thus he lived with relatives for most of the year, coming home to his village during the rainy season to help with farming chores. While away from home, he recalls spending his spare time playing soccer in the street with friends or going hunting. Their version of hunting is a little different from ours: He and his friends would whistle to the stray dogs lurking about and, after gathering five to six dogs, would hunt squirrels and rabbits, sharing the kill with the dogs! Modou and his siblings remember growing up in their village with nostalgia, especially the festivals with lots of singing and drumming. In particular, he thinks back on the coming-of-age ceremonies for boys aged nine to eleven. Generally, only male circumcision is practiced in Senegal, but in some areas in the south of the country, female genital mutilation is still the norm.

Modou went on to graduate from the University of Cheikah Anta Diop in Dakar, majoring in literature and philosophy. While his college years were intellectually and spiritually satisfying, financially things were very tough; he rarely had enough to eat or even a good place to live. After university, as a teacher of philosophy and French, life was a bit easier, but far from comfortable. The pay was meager, and, as is the Senegalese custom, he sent a fair chunk of his earnings to his parents. He often ran out of money before the month was over. Nowadays he reflects on the fact that although things were often very tough in Senegal, he was in a more spiritual place there than he is here, in this country, and was more accepting of what fate dealt him.

Senegal, like many West and North African countries, is predominantly Muslim. But Senegal is unique in that the overwhelming majority of Senegalese practice Sufism, the mystical branch of Islam. When Modou arrived in the America, three years after 9/11, in an intense climate of Islamophobia, he was hesitant to talk about his faith. However, he soon discovered that by revealing the tolerant Islam he knew, he was able to help his American friends achieve a more positive view of Islam.

Central to Senegalese Sufism is Ahmadou Bamba (1853–1921), a revered Gandhi-like figure who preached hard work, religious tolerance and nonviolent resistance to the French colonial occupation. Ahmadou Bamba survived torture and immense hardship at the hands of the French during two lengthy periods of exile, but he ultimately won their acceptance and admiration. He is regarded as a saint in Senegal, and every year, to honor his philosophy of tolerance and nonviolent resistance, celebrations are held in New York City, in Paris and throughout Senegal.

Modou's mother's words give insight into the Sufi worldview:

> Everything that exists has a soul and for that reason, everything deserves to be treated with respect and dignity. There is a spirit that lives in each plant, in each tree, in each flower, in each stone. Each animal, no matter how small, has a spirit.

In 1998, Modou met a dance student from Vermont who was on a visit to Senegal. She later returned to Senegal, and they married and settled in Dakar. After four years, at the urging of his wife, they moved to Vermont, seeking a better quality of life and more work opportunities.

Modou Nirone

Friends of Modou's relaxing after dance class.

After arriving in Vermont, Modou initially decided to pursue a master's degree at the University of Vermont, but to expedite the admission process, he chose instead to attend university in Montreal, where his Senegalese academic credits, being in the French system, were more easily transferable. However, commuting between classes in Montreal and home in Vermont on a weekly basis turned out to be time-consuming and humiliating. When he re-entered the U.S. after a week of classes in Canada, the rigorous, repetitious scrutiny he encountered at the border took its toll. Eventually he took a break from his studies and later completed a Master's in Education at the University of Vermont.

Over the years, Modou has taught French at middle schools in Williston, Waterbury, Stowe, and Warren and at Norwich University. He also co-taught a course in ethics at UVM. At Norwich University, he taught a course in cultural awareness to members of the Vermont National Guard. Specifically, he taught an introductory course in Senegalese culture and languages—Wolof and French—to Guard members who were about to deploy to Senegal as part of an American–Senegalese partnership and training program. The hope was that equipping Guard members with useful phrases and a basic understanding of local customs would ensure that the soldiers would be seen not as a hostile military presence, but rather as partners working together with Senegalese in areas of common interest. The program was very successful and was much appreciated by the guardsmen.

Modou lives in Morrisville (in Lamiolle County, 10 miles north of Stowe) and works as a counselor for Treatment Associates, Inc., a private organization that treats individuals who are struggling with mental health or substance abuse disorders. A life-long soccer player, he has also completed both the New York City Marathon and the Burlington City Marathon. He plays the balaphone, a type of xylophone that originated in West Africa, and he has recorded a CD with Burlington's legendary Gordon Stone. While he misses friends and family back in Senegal—not to mention the food and the music—he has made the adjustment to life here.

SOMALIA

Somalia is located on the east coast of Africa and occupies the area known as the Horn of Africa, the defining physical feature of Africa's east coast. The proximity of the "Horn" to the Arabian Peninsula creates a relatively narrow passageway for shipping traffic to and from the Red Sea, the Suez Canal and the Strait of Hormuz. Enhancing Somalia's strategic location is the fact that shipping lanes up and down the east coast of Africa naturally run close to Somalia's protruding coast for an extended stretch.

As a consequence of the chaotic state of the country after the 1991 civil war, Somalia's ability to protect its lucrative fishing grounds evaporated. The subsequent sharp increase in illegal fishing activity and the dumping of toxic waste in Somali waters led first to retaliatory attacks by local fishermen and their armed compatriots and then to the seeking out and capturing of foreign ships for ransom: in a word, piracy. The country's location provided direct, unchallenged access to shipping lanes, making it surprisingly easy for low-tech pirate activity to flourish.

In open boats, powered by outboard motors, pirates ranged far out to sea—100, 200 miles and more—in search of targets. Well-armed and equipped with boarding ladders and ropes, their typical MO was to attack ships early in the morning, surprising and overwhelming the unarmed crew. Over the years, this evolved into a lucrative enterprise: Recovering a ship, its cargo and crew usually involved ransoms in the millions of dollars. But by 2016, pirate activity had essentially been brought to an end, as military vessels from various countries, including the U.S., had begun patrolling the waters off the Somali coast.

As a country, one can say Somalia is a work in progress. True to the norm for many countries in the region, Somalia's current boundaries—and its very nationhood—were determined to a large extent by European powers. Its history prior to European intervention is exotic and complex, and since the written form of the language appeared only recently, its history is little known outside the country. For example, how well known is it that in the 1860s, Sultan Yusuf, the third Sultan of Gobroon, ushered the Gobroon Dynasty into its golden age?

In 1960, Somalia was granted independence from Italy. Beginning in the early 20th century, Italians began developing and settling the area around

Shanghai Old City in Mogadishu, a neighborhood favored by Europeans during the colonial era.

Mogadishu, Somalia's capital and largest city. Extensive infrastructure projects were carried out—roads, railways, schools, bridges, hospitals and churches were built—and banana plantations supported a thriving export trade with Europe. Relations with the local population were evidently constructive and mutually respectful, and by 1940 about 50,000 Italians were living in Somalia. However, relations with other European powers in the region were less cordial, and invasions and minor wars, not to mention World War II, continually redefined "ownership" of areas in the region. Today, terms like Italian Somaliland, British Somaliland and Jubaland are no longer relevant. In 1949, Italy's status in the region was given a brief revival, with the UN granting it trusteeship over its former domain, but on the condition that within 10 years, Somalia would become an independent country.

The initial years after independence were relatively peaceful, but increasingly, inter-ethnic strife began to manifest itself. An ill-advised border war (Ogaden War 1977–78) between Somalia and neighboring Ethiopia, which Somalia started and lost, further ramped up tensions between Somalia's two main groups, the farming-based Bantu people and the nomadic, cattle-tending Somali. Illustrating this, Bantu men were conscripted to fight in the war—a fight that was not their fight—with little or no training, leading to high casualty rates. The latter group, often referred to as Somali Somali, predate the Somali Bantu and are the dominant group. Bantus are descendants of slaves brought to the region from more southern areas (Tanzania, Mozambique and Malawi) by Arab slave traders in the 19th century and are assigned a lower status in Somalia. But both groups speak variations of the same language and both are Sunni Muslims. While Somali refugees in the United States are primarily Bantus, a significant percentage are Somali Somali as well. This is due to the fact that Somalia's troubles are less a matter of discord between these groups, and more a matter of inter-clan warfare among Somali Somalis themselves. Somali Bantus find themselves caught in the middle, marginalized and exploited by the warring parties.

In 1969, the president of Somalia was assassinated, and an army general, Siad Barre, became president. The early years of his leadership were characterized by various progressive and modernization initiatives, but after the disastrous Ogaden War, under increasingly dictatorial rule, his popularity declined, social gains were reversed and the economy faltered. In 1991 he was deposed, and the country descended into civil war, a war that

TSGT Terry Heimer/Wikimedia

Marine helicopter surveying Mogadishu residential districts for signs of militants.

Somali refugee in Kakuma Refugee Camp, Kenya.

is playing out to this day. Somali's internationally known author Nuruddin Farah characterizes of the state of the country in the years after the Ogaden experience and leading up to the civil war:

> Once our army came home vanquished, the defeat became an infestation in the body politic, eventually resulting in an implosion, which took the shape of an all-out war, a war on all and everyone, Somali killing Somali. With no faith in ourselves as a nation, we fragmented into blood communities and then further into smaller units. Civil wars erupt when a people are no longer in touch with their reality. In 1991 we lost touch with the reality of our Somaliness.

The destabilization brought on by the civil war and the attendant disruption of food production and distribution, particularly in the key grain-producing southern areas near Kismayo, led to a nationwide famine.

An international mission, led by the U.S., was put in place to help ensure fair distribution of food aid. On October 3, 1993, frustrated with the ruling warlords in Mogadishu, Army Rangers based on the outskirts of Mogadishu launched a raid to kidnap two lieutenants of Mohamed Farrah Aidid, the self-proclaimed leader of the country. Intended as a lightning-fast, surgical operation, the mission quickly degenerated into a nightmare of epic proportions: helicopters were shot down and American soldiers found themselves in a fight for their lives, trapped in a hostile city. Known by Americans as Black Hawk Down (film and book of the same name), and by Somalis as the Day of the Rangers, the resulting rescue operation lasted well into the next day. As horrific and humiliating as the ensuing battle was—18 Americans and 500–1,000 Somalis were killed—the two-day battle left a bitter legacy with consequences beyond Somalia. Stung by the debacle in Mogadishu, the United States, under President Clinton, subsequently cut back on aid and assistance in Africa. Thus, less than a year later, America failed to correctly assess and intervene in the Rwandan Genocide, something Clinton later apologized for on a visit to Rwanda.

For years, and up to the present, Somalia has been plagued by various Islamic extremist groups, mainly the al Qaida-related Al Shabab and ISIS.

CT Snow, Wikimedia

Somali armed jeep, known as a "technical."

148

Young Somalis in Berbera, Somalia.

While the United States has been providing limited military support to the legitimate, elected government, fighting and droughts continue to generate refugees and internally displaced persons. It is estimated that approximately half of the country's 12 million people suffer from serious food shortages.

Despite this gloomy assessment, Westerners who live and work in Somalia are optimistic about its future. Somalis are known for their resourcefulness and entrepreneurial skills, as shown by the fact that American Somalis own many businesses in the U.S., particularly in the Minneapolis area. Once security concerns are adequately addressed, the tourism potential of Somalia's beautiful landscape and endless sandy beaches can be realized.

Jared Gange

150

ABDULLAHI ADAMH

SOMALIA

Abdullahi was born in 1962 in Kismayo, a city on Somalia's southern coast, two years after Somalia won its independence from Italy. In the early post-colonial years when Abdullahi was a young boy, merchants from India, traders from Arab countries and a mix of Europeans lived harmoniously with the local native population in a warm and sunny climate on the sandy shores of the Indian Ocean. Abdullahi recalls:

> I am very proud of that time. Along the banks of the River Juba, we had banana plantations and our gardens produced many crops. We had so much livestock, and the local Bagiuni fishermen caught lots of fish. It was a very, very prosperity place: one part is the farm, the fish, livestock—everything! That was a good time for our young time.

Abdullahi started school when he was five. According to Muslim tradition, his first school was a Koranic school, one based on learning the Koran and the Arabic language. After three years of focusing on religion, he and other boys his age transitioned to a secular primary school.

Prior to 1972, the country's official language—Somali—did not exist in written form. Once writing was possible, an ambitious, nationwide campaign was launched to promote literacy, to spread the word, so to speak.

Remarkably, this was carried out primarily by boys about Abdullahi's age, 14 to 17. Accompanied by their teachers, they fanned out across the country and, over a period of four months, taught their countrymen (businessmen, farmers, even nomads) to read and write. Abdullahi graduated from high school in 1978.

But by the time Abdullahi had finished school, Kismayo's relaxed, prosperous way life was a thing of the past. Cattle herders from the drought-stricken north of the country—members of Somalia's dominant ethnic group—had migrated to the area, triggering disputes over land rights and water usage. Abdullahi and his fellow members of Somalia's disadvantaged ethnic group—the Bantus, often referred to as Somali Bantus—found themselves increasingly marginalized on their home turf. Fortunately for Abdullahi, he was never conscripted to fight in Somalia's disastrous border war (1982) with neighboring Ethiopia. Many Bantu men were sent into battle with little or no training; they were essentially cannon fodder.

Unable to find a job in Kismayo, and recently married to Sadia, Abdullahi decided to move to Marere, a village about 30 miles away. There, Sadia's father provided them with a plot of land to grow vegetables, and Abdullahi found a job with the local sugar factory, the Juba Sugar Project. Abdullahi was almost 19, Sadia 15.

Norwegian Refugee Council

UN Humanitarian Air Services plane approaching Dinsoor, central Somalia, 2017.

The years that followed were happy and productive for Abdullahi and his growing family. He enjoyed his job working with sugar cane irrigation, their two daughters were thriving, all was well. Abdullahi sums it up:

> I was expecting to live there the rest of my life. Because I had a good life there, I have my garden, I have my job. My wife's father left his big farm, mango trees, coconut trees, to us.

The increasing discrimination that Abdullahi and his fellow Bantus had experienced in Kismayo was bad enough, but what was to come was far worse. In the late 1980s, dissatisfaction with the country's longtime leader, Siad Barre, was evolving into civil war, with the country's two dominant clans (Daarood and Awiya) locked in a violent struggle for control of the country. Abdullahi, his village and his Bantu brethren were not party to this struggle, but they lost everything because of it. As the fighting raged, first one group, then the other, would sweep through Marere and the surrounding villages, taking whatever food and supplies they needed. Eventually, Abdullahi and his family felt they had no choice but to leave. Abdullahi describes their plight:

> Because when these group comes they take all what you have, food and everything. They rape the women, they beat and kill. We are in the middle, we don't have weapons. Every time you are expecting maybe this will end. But finally, when we have no food, nothing, everything they took, even our animals, we had a couple of goats, we flee.

They walked for three days to reach the relative safety of Kismayo. For three months they lived with Abdullahi's family. After scraping together some money, they continued walking, now south along the coast, to the Kenyan border. Keeping to the "bush" as much as possible—using the road was an invitation to be robbed, or worse—Abdullahi and Sadia carried their young daughters by day, sleeping on the ground at night. Occasionally, along the way, local inhabitants were able to sell or give them food. In some areas lions and hyenas were a concern, but the animal most feared was the human kind.

After walking for seven days, they reached the border. There, together with thousands of others fleeing Somalia, they waited to be registered and processed by UNHCR, the UN's primary agency for refugee assistance. After a month, Abdullahi's family was sent to Marafa Camp, near Kenya's

Selling spaghetti in Kakuma refugee camp.

famed beach resort, Mombasa, but a world away in comfort and safety. There they lived relatively uneventfully for about three years. Gardening supplemented their food rations, and camp residents were allowed to leave the camp for work in nearby towns, returning to the camp at the end of the work day. Eventually, rising concerns about the safety of the area's tourists led the Kenyan government to close the camp and relocate its inhabitants. Some of the very actors—the belligerents—from whom Abdullahi and his family had fled had also fled to Kenya and now lived among them. And it was the actions of these rogue individuals—some were armed—that posed a threat to area safety.

Abdullahi's family's new home was Kakuma. Located in Kenya's desert region of Turkana, Kakuma is an enormous camp, a city really. While not without its dangers and obvious drawbacks, Kakuma provided a significant degree of stability and safety for most of its residents. Be that as it may, life in a refugee camp is ultimately a dead-end existence. As a Kakuma resident from South Sudan expressed it, *You have no future, you are just waiting for your death.* However, for Abdullahi, his time there was a period of growth: he held gratifying, useful jobs. Working with aid agencies, he learned a great deal distributing food to camp residents and monitoring the health of young children. Perhaps most important, he learned English well, an asset that has been key to his success here.

154

In the camps, as the years pass, most refugees are sustained by the hope that one day they will be able to return home and resume their former lives. But in Kakuma, Somali elders—the respected authority figures for Somali Bantus—realized this was unlikely to happen. Thus, they told their people to abandon hope of returning home and to apply for resettlement in a third country—that is, not in Kenya and not back home in Somalia. Accordingly, UNHCR submitted their applications to various countries. As Abdullahi recalls:

> Our application they put everywhere. The United States accepted our application, because when they see how the Bantus are being treated in the country and they don't have the power to go back, because they don't have weapons and they were not fighting. They are the victims, real victims.

Thus, after 17 years as a refugee and 42 years old, Abdullahi arrived in America, in Phoenix, as it turned out. But after only four months, responding to requests for help from relatives already living in Vermont, he and his family moved to Burlington. Thus began his career as an interpreter and case worker for new arrivals and other refugees needing help who speak one of his four African languages; Arabic, Somali, Maay Maay and Swahili. Abdullahi's role is crucial in helping people fill out forms, apply for jobs, make medical appointments, and so on. Unfortunately, he finds he has very little use for his Italian. As a kid he learned the language watching movies: Italian films and the popularity of spaghetti are part of the legacy of Somalia's period as an Italian colony.

Today, at 55, Abdullahi has a good job and is a highly respected member of our Somali community. As a Muslim, he has been able to make the all-important pilgrimage to Mecca (in Saudi Arabia) and has made extended visits to both Malawi and Somalia, reconnecting with relatives and friends. While she speaks almost no English, Sadia is quite happy living here. Of their surviving four children—two died in refugee camps—their oldest lives with her husband and children in Utica, New York; their older son lives and works here in Burlington, and the younger boy has just moved to Utah to start college there. Their youngest, Hawa, is attending Middlebury College on a scholarship. Hawa is a member of *Muslim Girls Making Change*, a local youth slam poetry group dedicated to social justice through poetry. *MGMC* has performed around the country and won numerous awards.

156

|||||

FATUMA BULLE

SOMALIA

Frightened by explosions and gunfire nearby, seven-year-old Fatuma and her friends ran into the house. Inside, the girls crowded into a dark, windowless room and, together with about 20 adults, waited for the fighting to subside. They waited a day, perhaps two, Fatuma isn't sure. But she does remember a frightened soldier bursting into the house at one point—a soldier speaking a language they couldn't understand. Outside, angry voices demanded they turn the soldier over to them. When they did, the two Somalis escorting him were shot as they stepped outside, but the soldier wasn't hit. He tripped on a water jug on the front step and fell out of the line of fire. Fatuma doesn't know what happened to him after that.

The episode related above, or a version of it, took place between 1991 and 1993, but Fatuma was so young and so traumatized that she is unsure of the exact details. What we do know is that Somalia was embroiled in a civil war starting in 1991, and that, more specifically, on October 3–4, 1993, the event known as Black Hawk Down (called the Day of the Rangers by Somalis) took place in Mogadishu. Popularized by a book and movie of the same name, Black Hawk Down is the story of a daring pre-dawn raid in the middle of the city on October 3 by Army Rangers, which resulted in the shooting down of two Apache attack helicopters and the deaths of 18 Army

Rangers. Their bodies were dragged through the streets of Mogadishu. Meanwhile, surviving members of the assault team were in a fight for their lives, surrounded by armed militia and enraged locals. In a fierce battle, lasting through the night and into the next day, U.S. and Pakistani forces were able to rescue the trapped soldiers. During the firefight, hundreds of Somalis—perhaps more than a thousand—were killed.

The background to the above is that starting in 1992, the American military was in Somalia as part of a UN-sanctioned effort—dubbed Operation Restore Hope—to assist with the humanitarian effort responding to a devastating famine that was putting millions of Somalis at risk of starvation. Elite American and Pakistani troops, based on the outskirts of Mogadishu, along with soldiers from 15 other countries, were assigned the task of ensuring that relief supplies reached those in need. Clan-based militant groups were killing aid workers and seizing and selling the food to buy weapons; at one point it was estimated that 80% of the food failed to reach those in need. However, it bears mentioning that the relief effort, problematic as it was, is credited with saving at least 100,000 lives, perhaps two or three times as many.

Fatuma and her family are from Mogadishu. She had lived there her entire life and has pleasant memories of family time at Mogadishu's beaches, but during the civil war, everything changed. After surviving an assassination attempt—a bullet intended for her dad struck Fatuma instead—her parents fled Mogadishu, leaving Fatuma in the care of relatives. Today, over 25 years later, that bullet is still lodged in Fatuma's arm.

After the Black Hawk Down incident (or perhaps at another point during the civil war, we don't know for sure), Fatuma recalls that as she sat alone on the street "waiting for her [destroyed] house to come back," one of the passersby who was fleeing the city scooped her up and took her with him and his family.

As is typical for many refugees, Fatima grew up in a refugee camp: she arrived when she was about 7 and was 16 or 17 when she left. She spent those years in the sprawling complex of four UNHCR camps in the eastern Kenyan town of Dadaab (near the Somali border), transitioning to Kakuma camp (another refugee camp in Kenya) prior to being resettled in Burlington. One of the world's largest refugee camps, Dadaab had over 230,000 residents as of January 2018. Dadaab provided its residents with shelter and enough food but was far from safe, especially for women. As Fatuma related in a 2016 *Seven Days* article, *The camp wasn't safe for women*

Shutterstock

Busy day at the beach, Mogadishu.

because sexual assaults were common. You don't have firewood. You have to go to the forest, and you never know if you're going to be raped. On a positive note, she was able to attend school and learn English. While living in Dadaab, she was adopted by an older Somali man, Osman Bulle, who gave her the name Fatuma Bulle—her actual given names are Balkhiis and Bishaaro.

Fatuma arrived in Burlington in 2004, as part of a group of Somali Bantus who had been living for years in the Dadaab camps. As a single woman with no relatives in this country, during her first months here she lived with a local couple, Michael and Megan Wenrich. They recall that Fatuma adapted quickly to life in Vermont, and with her language skills—Fatuma speaks Swahili, the lingua franca of East Africa, as well as Maay Maay and Somali—she quickly got a job as an interpreter, helping other refugees transition to life in Vermont.

159

Drawing further on Kymelya Sari's 2016 article in *Seven Days*:

By 2007, Bulle felt ready to start her own family; she didn't want to be alone any longer. She married a Somali man she had known in the refugee camp, and he moved from Chicago to live with her in Vermont. But "life is full of surprises," Bulle said. Her husband turned out to be abusive.

"I remember a night ... my child's father was going to kill me with a pillow," she said. To calm him down, "I said, 'I love you,' and then he let me go," she said in a steady voice, as her eyes welled up. "He told me that if I told anybody, I'm not going to be alive."

It's rare in Somali Bantu culture for a woman to divorce her husband, Bulle said, so there was little support from her community. She tried to leave her husband because she didn't want her son to grow up in an unhealthy environment, but for months the elders dissuaded her from doing so, urging her to be patient.

Divorce: "They wouldn't let me do it. They stopped me many, many times," she said. "They are men. Men always side with the men. They don't listen to women." Her husband eventually agreed to a divorce to avoid a criminal charge after she reported him to the police for domestic abuse.

"Some people may look at her as someone who isn't respectful to the culture [because] she chose to leave her marital home," Thato Ratsebe, a female friend, said. "But over time, people have learned that, in fact, she made the best choices." Many victims of domestic violence wish they were as strong as Bulle, but "they just don't have the strength to stand up for themselves or step out," Ratsebe said.

After her divorce and now as a single parent, Fatuma struggled to continue her education. She switched from Champlain College to Burlington College because the latter would let her bring her young son, Ahmed, to class.

After graduating, Fatuma joined the Vermont Family Network support staff, facilitating contact between parents of children with disabilities— especially New American parents—and medical professionals. In addition to finding it daunting to deal with the health care system, refugee parents often resist admitting that their child has a disability, or that anything

Fatuma leading a focus group in Burlington.

can be done about it. In addition to her cultural bona fides, Fatuma has experience in this area, as her son has a learning disability.

In her mid-twenties, Fatuma decided to find out if her parents were alive, and if so, to reconnect with them. In 2010, she was able to fly to Ethiopia (Ethiopia borders Somalia and is home to thousands of Somali refugees), and by inquiring in refugee camps she learned her mother was alive and living in northern Somalia. When she visited her, Fatuma learned that her dad had survived too and was living in London. Her mother gave Fatuma his address, and the following year Fatuma showed up at his house. Fatuma recalls his reaction when he opened the door: *He was crying and calling his sister's name. He was sure I was his sister; he was sure I was dead. He had forgotten about me.* Only by showing him the bullet wound on her arm from long ago was Fatuma able to convince him that the tall woman standing before him was the same person as the seven-year-old daughter he had given up for dead.

In 2018, Fatuma remarried and moved to Brooklyn. She and her husband have satisfactory jobs, but Fatuma misses Vermont and her friends here. Ahmed is thriving and making progress in school now that he has a tutor.

SUDAN and SOUTH SUDAN

From its source in the highlands of East Africa, the Nile River flows north, breathing life into the drought-prone regions of South Sudan, Sudan and finally Egypt, before emptying into the Mediterranean Sea. As it passes through South Sudan, the Nile slows and spreads out across the landscape, forming a vast swamp, the Sudd. The Sudd expands and contracts seasonally: in a strong rainy season it covers an area five times the size of Vermont. When the rains end, the waters recede, leaving in their wake lush grasslands that support South Sudan's traditional cattle-raising cultures. With its furnace-like heat, unbearable numbers of mosquitos, crocodiles and annual food shortages, the Sudd is one of the last places we westerners would want to call home. But those who grew up there view it differently:

> It was an ideal childhood. I would not trade our homeland for any other place on Earth. It is the land of our ancestors, the land of our cattle and our vegetables, the land we pass on to our descendants. I never questioned that I would live forever in this Eden. (John Bul Dau, *God Grew Tired of Us*)

The Sudd's confusing network of waterways and mats of floating vegetation were a profound hindrance for British explorers—and Roman soldiers long before them—traveling up the Nile seeking the river's source. Only by circumventing the Sudd was it possible to continue upstream to Lake Victoria and the river's headwaters.

In 1987, the idyllic existence described above came under threat, as well-armed fighters from the north of the country attacked and destroyed southern villages, killing, raping and abducting their inhabitants. The attacks tended to occur at night, and in the ensuing chaos, children were often separated from their parents. Some ran away, while others were captured and forced to join their attackers as child soldiers. The children who escaped the initial attacks, separated from their families and afraid to return to their destroyed villages, began a desperate wandering from place to place. Joining with others who had suffered the same fate, they coalesced into larger groups. Thus, the stage was set for one of the most unique and horrific migrations in history. Thousands of young boys, along with a few girls and some adults, wandered from place to place for years, constantly on

162

Life along the Nile River in South Sudan.

the lookout for enemy fighters, scrounging for food and water, vulnerable to snakes, hyenas and lions, all the while looking for a safe haven. They became known as the Lost Boys of Sudan and are considered to be among the most traumatized victims of war the world has ever seen. Estimates of the number of Lost Boys vary from 26,000 to considerably more.

After years of wandering, the surviving children—it is estimated that about half died from their ordeal—finally reached safety in Kakuma Refugee Camp in Kenya, where they languished for years before being permanently resettled in other countries. In 2001, the United States resettled about 4,000 Lost Boys, two of whom are featured in this book. While the story of the Lost Boys of Sudan provides some insight into the struggles faced by the people of South Sudan, it is an unfortunate fact that their struggles represent only a fraction of the suffering the people of South Sudan have been forced to endure and continue to endure.

Prior to 2011, the country of Sudan was huge—the largest in Africa—comprising an area about the size of the United States east of the

Celebrating South Sudan's independence from Sudan, 2011.

Mississippi. In 2011, a popular referendum was held in the geographically and ethnically distinct southern portion of Sudan. It resulted in an almost unanimous verdict, 98%, in favor of secession. The new country of South Sudan was duly formed, becoming Africa's 54th independent nation. For South Sudanese, this was the fulfillment of a long-held, and hard-earned dream.

The remaining, significantly larger and more populous northern portion retains the name Sudan. Thus, South Sudan and a now smaller Sudan together encompass the land area held by the Sudan that existed before 2011. The inhabitants of the north are primarily of Arab origin, speak Arabic and are overwhelmingly Muslim. The total population of Sudan is about 40 million, and its capital, Khartoum, with about seven million inhabitants, is located at the confluence of the two main stems of the Nile, the White Nile and the shorter Blue Nile. Khartoum and its two satellite cities, Omdurman and North Khartoum, are clustered together along the banks of the two rivers.

South Sudan is a clan-based society of great ethnic and linguistic diversity: there are approximately 60 ethnic groups and 80 languages and dialects, with English widely used by the educated elite. In stark contrast to their former countrymen to the north, South Sudanese practice various Christian or African religions. The capital city, Juba, with a population of about 500,000, is located in the far south of the country, only a short drive from the border with Uganda. Like Sudan's capital Khartoum, and Egypt's Cairo, Juba is spread out along the life-giving Nile River. The population of South Sudan is about 12 million.

Of the many clans and sub-clans in South Sudan, the two main clans, the Dinka and the smaller Nuer, comprise about 40% and 15% of the population, respectively. The Dinka and the Nuer have long had a fraught relationship, and much of the hardship and violence South Sudan has experienced after independence is a direct result of bad blood between the Dinka, the Nuer and the other clans. Among these cattle-raising societies, skirmishes are typically triggered by disputes over grazing lands, water usage and cattle theft.

Dreamstime

Khartoum, capital of Sudan, and the Nile River at sunset.

Since the creation of Sudan by the British in 1956, the northern and southern regions have been at odds, with almost continuous fighting between the Arab-dominated north and the traditionally African southern region. Two protracted civil wars were fought, the First Sudanese Civil War (1955–1972) and the Second Civil War (1983–2005). Sadly, since achieving independence, South Sudan has been ravaged by its own civil war, pervasive inter-clan conflicts, drought and famine.

For example, in 2013 a dispute between the president and his vice-president led to a civil war wherein over a million South Sudanese were internally displaced and many thousands became refugees. Compounding an already challenging political landscape is the fact that Sudan and South Sudan disagree over the distribution of revenue from the region's significant oil reserves. The oil fields lie along the border between the two countries. South Sudan lays claim to the lion's share, but Sudan controls the essential

John Wollwerth, Dreamstime

Women carrying roofing material, Torit, South Sudan.

166

Torben Nissen

South Sudanese fisherman at home wih his wife and child.

pipelines that carry the oil to Port Sudan on the Red Sea, a thousand miles distant. The government of South Sudan is completely dependent on its oil revenues.

South Sudan has potential tourist revenue from its abundant wildlife—especially noteworthy is the annual antelope migration in the undeveloped Boma National Park, an area almost as large as Vermont. The country's grasslands and rainforest support healthy populations of buffalo, gazelle, elephant, zebra, lion and leopard, but given the weak economy and the generally poor security situation, prospects for increased development and tourism in the near term remain dim.

Chol (left) and Atem with his daughter, Aluel.

‖‖‖

ATEM AROK DENG, CHOL KIIR ATEM

SOUTH SUDAN

Atem and Chol were born in the village of Kongor in southern Sudan. They have known each other since they were about six years old. In those days Kongor was a thriving community consisting of thousands of huts spread over a large area. The entire population belonged to the Dinka ethnic group, the predominant clan of southern Sudan. Dinkas are subsistence farmers but also adhere to the tradition of "cattle keeping." Prized for both milk and meat, but primarily for milk, cattle were everything to the Dinka. More than a source of nourishment, cattle represent status for the Dinka and are the measure of a family's wealth.

Every year after the seasonal rains, Atem and Chol, along with the other boys, would move their families' cattle to "cattle camps," where the cattle fattened on the lush grass that sprang up every year after the spring floods receded. Living on their own, away from their parents, enjoying their independence and bearing the responsibility for herds of cattle, Dinka boys like Atem and Chol found this to be a happy time. According to Atem, there were so many cattle that they were "uncountable."

The Dinka way of life, sustained by vegetable farming and the keeping of cattle, offered a stable and fulfilling existence. By Western standards this was no easy life: periods of food uncertainty, extreme heat and swarms of

Joerg Boethling

Dinka boy relaxing with his family's cattle.

mosquitos were facts of life. But for Atem and Chol, now in their mid-thirties and well established here in Vermont, the life they led as children will forever be a part of them, and they miss it beyond measure.

In 1989, when Atem and Chol were seven years old, their peaceful existence was brutally snuffed out. Attacked in the middle of the night by well-armed soldiers, the defenseless villagers of Kongor scattered in panic. Many were killed in the massacre that followed. Homes were looted, the thatched roofs torched, cattle slaughtered and families split apart. The civil war between the Muslim, Arab-dominated northern part of Sudan and the Christian, Nilotic-speaking southern part, which had been raging since 1983, had made its way to them.

During the attack and the ensuing confusion, Atem and Chol and many others fled into the nearby "bush," as they call the uninhabited counrtyside. Separated from their parents and afraid to return home, they and others, mostly young boys, began a desperate journey to safety, away from the soldiers. Not knowing where to go, they first headed west but then turned east, toward Ethiopia, where they were told Sudanese fighters friendly to their people were based. As they walked, they were joined by traumatized children from other villages, swelling their ranks into the hundreds; eventually they were about a thousand. Aided by the few adults

170

who were with them, the children were somehow able to find enough food to keep most of them alive by foraging, hunting and begging. Finding water was a constant problem; sometimes they resorted to drinking urine or sucking water out of mud. As they walked, many succumbed to starvation, dehydration or sickness. Some were taken by lions, others were captured or killed by enemy Arab fighters or by hostile tribes. Finally, after two months of walking, the survivors reached the Blue Nile (the major tributary of the Nile) and swam across to Ethiopia and safety.

Atem and Chol—along with thousands of boys with similar stories—spent four years in Ethiopia. Their initial, pitifully primitive circumstances gradually improved, as the United Nations and other aid agencies responded to their plight and created a proper refugee camp, called Pinyudo. Because these young boys had lost touch with their families and were so far from home, aid workers began referring to them as the Lost Boys. The name stuck and to this day veterans of this bizarre journey are known as the Lost Boys of Sudan.

During their years in Ethiopia, the boys enjoyed a measure of safety and were given clothing, blankets and enough food to survive. They organized, the older boys looking after the younger ones, the healthy caring for the sick. They scrounged logs and branches to improve their shelters, and the fish they caught bolstered their meager rations. Atem and Chol regard this period as a relatively happy time, as their basic needs were met, and they were no longer in physical danger. But with little understanding of hygiene, and living in filthy circumstances, children continued to sicken and die from malaria and typhoid fever. The boys learned to dig graves and perform simple funeral rites for their friends. But lacking proper digging tools, they were able to dig only very shallow graves: at night the boys could hear lions and hyenas digging up the fresh graves.

As satisfactory as their lives in Ethiopia may or may not have been, when Ethiopia descended into civil war in 1991, the camp leaders realized that they, and the children in their care, were in grave danger. The decision was made to return to Sudan, but in the midst of preparing to leave, they were caught by surprise and attacked by soldiers using tanks and machine guns. Fleeing for their lives, the boys found their way blocked by the fast flowing Gilo River, a river notorious for its numerous, large crocodiles. With no bridge and no boats, their only way to safety was to swim across. Good swimmers like Atem and Chol had a reasonable chance of making it to the other side, but many boys drowned. Others were shot or were caught by crocodiles: the river ran red with blood. This horrific event, known as the Gilo River Massacre, is depicted below in a drawing, by one of the survivors.

Once across the Gilo River, with only the clothes on their backs, the survivors found themselves in their home country, but once again exposed to Sudan's civil war. As they trekked through southern Sudan, now numbering in the thousands, they were better organized than before, and, more importantly, they were monitored and assisted by the Red Cross and the UN. However, stragglers were prone to kidnapping, food was absolutely minimal and wild animals were an ever-present threat. This chapter of their ordeal had the added feature of aerial bombardment by northern Sudanese forces.

Despite several attempts to settle in towns along the way, continual harassment by Arab fighters from the north kept the Lost Boys on the move. Ultimately the decision was made for them to cross into Kenya. About 60 miles south of the border, in the dusty, bone-dry region of northwest Kenya known as the Turkana, the boys' wandering days finally ended. Near the village of Kakuma Town, the UNHCR (the UN Refugee Agency), had begun building facilities to handle refugees fleeing violence in Sudan and Somalia, and Atem and Chol would spend the next nine years

Drawing by Mac Anyat

Ethiopian soldiers forcing Sudanese Lost Boys into the Gilo River, 1991.

Torben Nissen

Kakuma Refugee Camp, Kenya, home for Atem and Chol for nine years.

in Kakuma Refugee Camp. They arrived when they were 11 years old and left when they were 20. The total number of Lost Boys is thought to be about 26,000, but by the time the last survivors arrived at Kakuma, their numbers were halved.

As refugees from Sudan and Somalia continued to pour into Kakuma, the camp swelled to one of the largest refugee camps in the world. Even today, Kakuma remains an important refuge for those fleeing conflict in Somalia, Burundi, Ethiopia, Congo and Sudan. As of February 2017, it was home to over 165,000 refugees.

When Atem and Chol were cleared to leave Kakuma for the U.S., they flew directly to Burlington, and within a week they were enrolled in high school, Atem in Burlington and Chol in Winooski. A few weeks after their arrival, Atem and Chol started working at Preci Manufacturing, a Winooski company that manufactures precision components for the aerospace, defense and electronics industries. Eighteen years later, they are still employed at Preci. Both "Boys" went on to finish college, Atem at the University of Vermont (social work) and Chol at Lyndon State College (marketing). Atem lives in South Burlington with his wife and two young daughters. Chol has been back to Kakuma several times, and in 2017 he married a women he had gotten to know there. His wife is now living with relatives in nearby Uganda while Chol works to obtain her visa so she can join him here.

‖‖‖

Peter Garang Deng
SOUTH SUDAN

At the age of seven Peter decided to run away. His father had died two years before, and his mother died when Peter was only eight months old. After their father died, Peter and his two older sisters moved in with relatives. Sadly, daily beatings became the norm for Peter. On many days he was given no food. As his father had foreseen as he lay dying:

> My son, this is a desert world, a world where relatives do not take good care of children that do not belong to them. If you fall down and can't pick yourself up, you will become history.

This is the story of a remarkable young boy who *was* able to pick himself up. His drive for an education sustained him, and he is now a well-educated, successful young man living in Burlington.

At a very early age, his father began telling him his family's history and instructing him in the ways of their clan, the Dinka-Bor. In particular, he told and retold the story of his courtship of Peter's mother. Despite his deep respect for clan traditions, Peter's father, the oldest of 10 kids, broke tradition by letting his younger brothers marry before he did, because he was waiting for a certain woman in a nearby village to become eligible. Nyakueth, the village beauty, in accordance with tradition, had to wait

Typical Dinka settlement, under drought conditions.

until her older sisters were married before she could marry. Eventually they were able to marry and lived together happily until her untimely death.

Peter's father was a village boy, but he was at home in the nearby city of Juba, and there he made his living and provided for his family. After Peter's mom died, the family moved back to their village. Cities and towns are home to beggars and orphans, and seeing so many orphans profoundly affected Peter's dad. He helped them as much as he could and repeatedly impressed upon his young son the need to help those in need, particularly children. At the time, Peter was impatient with his father's stories of orphans, even as his father warned him that this could be his fate someday.

Indeed, his father's grim prediction came to pass. After his father died, Peter and his sisters moved back and forth between their aunt's house and their uncle's house. It was hard for Peter to tell which was worse. At his aunt's he was fed but also beaten and had to do most of the chores. At his uncle's, he was beaten by his uncle's wife and deprived of food. His uncle, while good to him, was ineffective in preventing his wife's abuse of Peter. To stave off starvation, Peter was sometimes able to get food from members of his sub-clan, the Penn, but there were days when he didn't eat at all. In Peter's words:

I adopted a plan of eating then skipping a few days before eating again, and eventually I trained my body to be able to sustain itself on this diet. It worked pretty well.

His grandmother was so distressed by Peter's suffering that she begged the gods to end her life. The gods soon answered her prayers, and one day she fell dead in front of Peter, blood coming out of her mouth. His uncle was so distressed by this that he, too, decided he was ready to die and did so soon thereafter. As Peter observes:

Though many westerners have trouble believing this, when traditional Dinka men and women call on the gods to end their lives, it will happen. And once you begin to die, nothing can cure you. This is what happened to my grandmother and my uncle.

After the death of his uncle, Peter realized that things were only going to get worse, so he and his sisters decided to move back in with their aunt. In fairly quick succession both sisters married and moved out; it would be eight years before he saw them again.

Joerg Boethling

The Nile River flows through Juba, capital of South Sudan.

When his sisters left, life truly became a nightmare. Sitting on the roadside one day, utterly despondent, as Peter watched children cheerfully rush-ing by on their way to school, he decided that he too would go to school and have a happy life. In traditional Dinka culture, schooling was held in low regard; it served mainly as a place to send problem kids, thus starting them off on a path away from home and away from their home village, so as not to besmirch the family's reputation. Thus his aunt, regarding Peter as worthless, was happy to send him to school. On his first day he arrived naked, much to the amusement of the other children.

School was the turning point in Peter's life. He was an excellent student! His academic ability would become his ticket to success. He was given writing materials and encouragement from his teachers. Soon he was tutoring his classmates in math; he got them to bring him food, because the only way to really learn was on a full stomach. His art projects earned him praise. A year passed. But since the beatings at home continued and he was still hungry much of the time, Peter decided to run away: *I realized I would have to leave my village to truly get ahead.*

Thus one day, Peter, only seven years old, hitched a ride on a truck and made his way to New Cush, a camp for internally displaced Sudanese. Schools were better in New Cush, and a distant relative took him under his wing. Getting enough to eat was no longer a problem because the land there is very fertile; sorghum, maize, peanuts and other food crops were plentiful. But life wasn't completely without problems. Local inhabitants, resenting the camp dwellers' relative prosperity, would regularly shoot at the camp from the surrounding hills. Seeing people killed became a normal experience for Peter.

When he was twelve, Peter moved on to Kakuma Camp in nearby Kenya. This enormous refugee camp in the parched desert region of Turkana is home (as of 2018) to about 185,000 Somali and South Sudanese refugees. Kakuma means "nowhere" in Swahili. Starvation rations, combined with clashes between the locals and camp residents—and among the refugees themselves—aggravate an already difficult existence. At Kakuma Peter registered with UNHCR, and in 2006, after six years of waiting, he was called for an interview, a major step on the path to receiving the green light to immigrate to America.

In the meantime, he had attended college in Kenya and was on the verge of becoming a Kenyan citizen when his clearance to move to the U.S. came through. He jumped at the chance, and after a rough start in Burlington, he soon found his way. His college education from Kenya counted for little here, and his first job was as a janitor at Fletcher Allen.

In Peter's words:

> You cannot keep the same dignity when you are outside your home country. You do what you have to do to survive. I became the underdog within the marginalized community here.

After a series of menial jobs, and plagued by persistent discrimination from his bosses, Peter realized he had to get a college degree to break the cycle of jobs that were getting him nowhere. He tried to influence others— friends from South Sudan—to go back to school as well, but as Peter notes:

> People who have never had money have a hard time leaving the jobs they have, and the money they are earning, even temporarily, to get an education and to get a better job.

But Peter broke the cycle and entered Champlain College, receiving his degree in 2011. The following year he completed his MBA (Plymouth State University) to the surprise of his advisor, who didn't think it possible to complete the program in a year. He plans to get a second MBA, specializing in finance. He speaks five languages and is learning two more.

Peter has a tax preparation business in Burlington, and in South Sudan he owns a money transfer business, a transportation service (Peter Deng Express) and, as of summer 2016, a small hotel near Juba, on the border with Uganda. As if that weren't enough, he also runs a school for orphaned children through his foundation, Deng Opportunities Foundation. Thus, when tax season winds down after mid-April and his clients are taken care of, Peter heads back to South Sudan for several months to meet with his employees and check on his various businesses.

Peter has written about his life in his book *Lost Generation, the Story of a Sudanese Orphan*. It is available from his website, www.peterdeng.com or www.nsjof.org

His next book, due out this year (2019), compares the cultural practices of local refugee groups with American cultural norms. The different approaches to socializing, punctuality, the role of women, child rearing and conflict resolution are explained. As Peter puts it: *It's about understanding your neighbor's culture.*

AHMED KHATIB

SYRIA

In 2012, on the advice of his older brother, Ahmed, his wife Mahasen and their young daughter fled their home in Aleppo to safety in nearby Turkey.

Civil war was tearing the country apart and Aleppo was especially hard hit. Across the country cities were being destroyed, and many areas were without water, electricity or medical services. Anyone with means was at risk of being kidnapped and held for ransom.

By bribing the soldiers stationed at the border, Ahmed and Mahasen were able to cross into Turkey at Kilis, a border town and the closest safe place for those fleeing northern Syria. They stayed there a few days with Mahasen's parents, who themselves had fled Syria only 11 days earlier, but the volatility and inherent danger of living so close to the war zone prompted Ahmed to move his family farther into Turkey, to the larger city of Gaziantep. A resourceful guy with some savings, Ahmed did not consider himself a refugee—being dependent on an aid organization for his food and shelter was not something he was willing to entertain. Thus, soon after arriving in Gaziantep, knowing no one and speaking no Turkish, Ahmed set out to find a place to live. Incredibly, almost immediately he met a local man who not only spoke Arabic but also had a tiny, one-room apartment they could rent and knew his father! Smoothing the transition further was the fact that Gaziantep is very similar to Aleppo, both architecturally and culturally. As one local puts it, "Aleppo and Gaziantep are in fact twin cities. Just visit the bazaar (marketplace) of both, and you will see the similarity."

About six months into their stay, with the war in Syria showing no signs of ending, Ahmed gave up on any immediate hope of returning to Syria and realized it was time for him to find a job. Initially he found work in construction, something he was familiar with from home, but he soon transitioned to a better-paying job delivering coal. After a shaky start— carrying 50-pound loads of coal up flights of stairs is not done "lightly"— Ahmed adapted to this new line of work. He and his crew delivered 12 tons of coal every day, and for this they were well paid, as few were willing and able to handle the job's physical demands.

As someone who has fled his country fearing for his life, Ahmed's case is unusual because he returned—the war still raging—several times. Ahmed was able to make the 75-mile trip to his ailing father and, on one trip, brought him to doctors in Turkey, later returning him home. As before, bribes at the border and at roadside checkpoints made these trips possible.

Ahmed was born in 1979, the youngest of 10 children. His father was a lawyer and a teacher, and his mother, as is the tradition, took care of the children and the household. His family was relatively well off, and Ahmed had a happy upbringing in Kufer Hamrah, a town about 15 minutes from Aleppo. He studied engineering at Aleppo University for four years but left before completing his fifth year to begin working full time. After leaving university, Ahmed worked in construction, real estate development and marketing.

Syria is an ancient country with a fabled past. Aleppo and the capital, Damascus, are two of the oldest continuously inhabited cities in the world, and evidence of civilization in the region dates back to 10,000 BC. Not surprisingly, Syria possesses a vast trove of archeological sites and treasures. Over the centuries, many cultures and empires have come and gone: Phoenicians, Assyrians, Babylonians, the Greek Macedonian Empire, Armenians, the Roman Empire, Mongols and the Ottoman Empire. As a Syrian friend of Ahmed's puts it:

Syria was beautiful. Syria was everybody's destination in Middle East. When you said you were from Syria, when you went to Saudi Arabia or you went to Egypt, they look up to you, because you are supposed to be educated, you are supposed to be smart. And now it's opposite: you are embarrassed to say you are from Syria.

Dinosmichail, Dreamstime

The medieval citadel of Aleppo, one of the oldest and largest castles in the world.

With the collapse of the Ottoman Empire at the end of World War I, France intervened militarily in Syria, and until the end of World War II, France was the League of Nations (precursor to the United Nations) Mandate of Syria, administering both Syria and neighboring Lebanon.

After gaining independence in 1946, Syria experienced periods of political instability, marked by a series of coups, but from 1971 to the onset of the current civil war (2011) the country enjoyed a stable but very repressive period, first under Hafez al-Assad (1971–2000), followed by his son Bashir al-Assad, who remains in power as of this writing.

Sadly, in Syria today, the stability referred to above has been replaced by the chaos of a devastating civil war: the repressive rule of the past would be a welcome relief from present conditions. The cause? The Arab Spring, if not the cause, was the trigger. The Arab Spring traces its origin to Tunisia, where in December 2010, a street vendor set himself on fire, protesting treatment

Smallcreative, Shutterstock

After three years of fighting, the city of Homs lies in ruins.

he had received from local police. Fueled by widespread dissatisfaction with Tunisia's corrupt and ineffective government, his death sparked violent protests throughout the country. Similar protests spread quickly eastward across North Africa and the Middle East. This wave of essentially pro-democracy, anti-authoritarian protests had profound consequences for the region. Within a month the Tunisian government had fallen, by February the Egyptian and Jordanian governments were ousted and the first protests in Kuwait, Morocco and Lebanon were under way. By late April, Syrian protesters' demands—for freedom of the press, freedom of speech, political parties *and* President Assad's resignation—were being met with maximum force.

As a spontaneous movement with no pre-existing organization or dedicated resources, the Arab Spring's innovative use of social media was effective in planning and carrying out protests, marches and other actions. If the Arab Spring started suddenly, taking the world by surprise, it died down quickly as well, with any unresolved issues no longer giving rise to civil unrest. But Syria is a tragic exception; eight years after the Arab

Spring first reached Syria, the country remains embroiled in a horrific civil war. The brutal, murderous response by the Syrian army to the initial nonviolent protests served only to strengthen opposition to Bashir Assad's authoritarian regime, and within a few months the country was in a civil war of mind-boggling complexity—a conflict that has created a humanitarian crisis of biblical proportions. As of late 2018, approximately 10 million people—out of a total population of 18–20 million—have fled the country. The military operations that liberated Homs and Raqqa have left these formerly thriving cities almost totally destroyed. The conflict has long ceased to be an internal matter, as Russia, the United States, Iran and various non-state actors have become involved. Ominously, particularly from a Western perspective, the war in Syria provided fertile soil for the growth and strengthening of ISIS, the *Islamic State of Iraq and Syria*.

As the war at home dragged on and worsened, living in Turkey without full legal status began to wear thin for Ahmed and Mahasen. As undocumented residents, it was impossible for Ahmed and his family to settle into a normal life. He was unable to own property or start a business,

Smallcreative, Shutterstock

Aerial view of Aleppo, showing war damage and the ancient citadel.

185

and as a Syrian, he repeatedly came under scrutiny. Thus, in 2015, he applied for resettlement in the United States, and after the usual round of interviews followed by long periods of waiting, his family was granted permission to emigrate to America. In January 2017, Ahmed, Mahasen and their three children (the two boys were born in Turkey) flew from Istanbul to Washington, D.C., and from there to New York, where they spent their first night in this country. The next day they traveled by taxi to Vermont, arriving in a bitterly cold, snow-covered Rutland at midnight. Mahasen burst into tears, horrified at where they had ended up. Her first comment was: *We left war and now we are in hell, a cold hell!* But their apartment was warm and the welcome they received from locals even warmer.

The local volunteer group *Rutland Welcomes* had been preparing for months to receive Syrian refugees, and thanks to their efforts, Ahmed's family and the two other Syrian families who relocated to Rutland probably benefitted from as smooth a transition as is possible for families experiencing an abrupt switch from the known to the unknown.

Two years into their lives here, Ahmed regards Rutland as home. "I feel like it's my town now," he says. Not one to dwell on his material losses—his

Jared Gange

From left to right, Mustafa, Mohamed, Ahmed, Mahasen and Dania at home in Rutland, December 2018.

Caleb Kenna

Members of the volunteer group Rutland Welcomes out in force, welcoming Rutland's third Syrian family's arrival, June 2017.

home and property in Aleppo, his investment in their apartment in Turkey—Ahmed is completely focused on providing for his family and succeeding here in America. He has a good job in quality control for a local window and door supplier and is a valued employee. In another year he will have paid off his debt to the U.S. government for the cost of his family's move from Turkey to Rutland. Their children have adapted to life here and are fluent in English. They own a car and Ahmed is teaching Mahasen to drive.

The loss of property is one thing, but losing contact with family—being unable to spend time together—is another matter altogether. Ahmed's mother is now living in Turkey, and he would like to bring her to Rutland, but under our government's current rules (as of 2019) for Syrian refugees, she is not eligible to apply for a visa. They are in contact with family members still in Syria by phone and by Facebook, but actually seeing each other is not a possibility at present.

Asked what they would like to be able to do here, Mahasen and Ahmed first respond that they would like to go to Florida, but upon further reflection, their wish would simply be to spend some warm summer days at a nearby lake.

TIBET

Located on an arid, high-altitude plateau, on the other side of the formidable Himalayan mountain range from India, Tibet has a fabled past as a remote and inaccessible land. Its unique culture and the adherence of its inhabitants to a little-known form of Buddhism have added to its mystique. The Tibetan plateau is both high and enormous: it spans an area about one-quarter the size of the United States, with an average elevation of over 15,000 feet. Its vast, treeless landscapes, interrupted here and there by nomad encampments and grazing yaks, are surprisingly beautiful. Moving across expanses of green and yellow grass, under a cloudless blue sky, the traveler is treated to changing hues of lavender and grey on nearby hills, an occasional lake and views of the icy Himalayan peaks—the world's tallest—that define the southern horizon.

Tibetan Buddhism originated in India, and various forms of it are practiced in Mongolia, Bhutan, India and throughout the Tibetan diaspora. This tradition places great emphasis on the importance of the lama—a guru, or teacher—and monastic life. At one point there were over 6,000 monasteries in Tibet, and each family was expected to send at least one child to monastery. The concept of incarnate lineage is a key aspect of Tibetan Buddhism. In this tradition, lamas, including the Dalai Lama, live on through successive reincarnations.

The Dalai Lama is the spiritual and political leader of the Tibetan people and the pre-eminent embodiment of a religious teacher for Tibetans. After the death of the 13th Dalai Lama in 1933, according to the Tibetan tradition, a team of high monks was dispatched across Tibet to locate the deceased Dalai Lama's reincarnation. Four years later, in 1937, a two-year-old peasant boy in a remote village in northeastern Tibet successfully passed a series of difficult tests, confirming that he was the reincarnation of the previous Dalai Lama. At age five, he was officially enthroned as the 14th Dalai Lama. Today, at 83, though he is no longer living in Tibet, Tenzin Gyatso, as he is known, continues to be the revered spiritual leader of all Tibetans, both inside Tibet and in Tibetan communities all over the world.

Over the centuries, Tibet's degree of autonomy and independence has waxed and waned, particularly with regard to neighboring China's ability to exert its power, but also with respect to the British, who invaded Tibet in

The iconic building of Tibet, Lhasa's Potala Palace, former home of the Dalai Lama.

1903, capturing the capital, Lhasa, before recalling its invasion force to India, in 1904. But for all intents and purposes, Tibet was a closed land, steeped in mystery. Western explorers in the late 18th and early 19th centuries found it basically impossible to enter Tibet. A famous breakthrough was the surprise arrival of two destitute Europeans who staggered into Lhasa in 1946. The two were Austrian mountain climbers who had escaped from a British internment camp in northern India several years earlier. Being part of a German expedition, they had the misfortune to find themselves in (then) British India when World War II broke out and were consequently detained. One of the men, Heinrich Harrer, became a tutor to the teenage Dalai Lama, greatly enhancing the worldview of the future leader of Tibet. Harrer's book, *Seven Years in Tibet,* has been made into a movie starring Brad Pitt.

About this time, Tibet's traditional way of life, and its isolation and autonomy, were about to come to an end. In 1950, when Mao Zedong emerged as the undisputed leader of China, he promptly laid claim to Tibet. The following year, representatives of the Tibetan government signed the so-called *Seventeen Point Agreement* drawn up by China, the first point of which states, "the Tibetan people shall return to the family of the Motherland, the People's Republic of China." In contrast to this profoundly objectionable first point, other points of the agreement clearly affirm Tibetan autonomy and the unaltered role of the Dalai Lama. The agreement was controversial from the outset and has been strongly disputed and rejected by Tibetans ever since.

After the signing of the agreement, it initially appeared that Tibetans' traditional way of life would be preserved, but when the Chinese began to forcibly implement land reforms, rebellions and uprisings (with some help from the CIA) sprang up across the country. Ultimately, Tibetan resistance was for naught, and by 1959 Tibet was firmly under Chinese control. Thus, in March of 1959, the 24-year-old Dalai Lama, fearing capture by the Chinese, escaped to India on horseback with his entourage under dramatic and desperate circumstances. A massive exodus followed; countless thousands, rich and poor, young and old, fled their homes to safety in India, most never to return.

Today, 60 years later, it is estimated that as many ethnic Tibetans live outside Tibet as within its borders. Vigorous suppression by the occupying Chinese of traditional Tibetan culture and religion, a massive influx of

Jared Gange

On the circuit of Mount Kailash, a mysterious mountain sacred to both Tibetan Buddhists and Hindus.

Overlooking the city of Shigatse from Tashi Lungpo Monastery.

Han Chinese into Tibet, as well as the more or less complete exclusion of Tibetans from significant participation in the economic and political life of their country, have all but destroyed a Tibet acceptable to most Tibetans. Tibet is today a province of the People's Republic of China and is known as Xizang, or the Tibet Autonomous Region.

Over the years, the governments of India and Nepal have done a commendable job of taking in Tibetan refugees. The Indian government has donated large tracts of land in southern India to Tibetan refugees. Over the years, Tibetans have built a number of large, authentically Tibetan communities totaling approximately 37,000 people. The Dalai Lama resides in Dharamshala, a town in India's northern foothills. Dharamshala is the headquarters of the Tibet Government in Exile, as well as home to many Tibetan exiles.

While India and Nepal have been very welcoming to displaced Tibetans, neither country grants them citizenship. Therefore, Tibetan refugees *and* their children and grandchildren—born in India or Nepal—are technically stateless. This was the background for the Immigration Act of 1990, which provided for 1,000 U.S. visas—via lottery—for Tibetans living in India and Nepal. Burlington, among 22 U.S. cities, including Austin, Madison,

191

Minneapolis and Seattle, was chosen as a resettlement site, and in 1992, 23 Tibetans arrived here. Lottery winners were not allowed to bring their families with them, the plan being to allow family members to come to the U.S. after two years. As it turned out, five years passed before families were allowed to reunite.

Today there are about 150 Tibetans living in the Burlington area; almost all are here directly or indirectly through the Tibetan Resettlement Project lottery program. The community is tightly knit and thriving. The level of employment and home ownership is high, and the next generation is getting a good education; many have graduated from college or are currently enrolled. There are approximately 25,000 Tibetans living in the U.S.; New York City and Minneapolis are the two largest communities.

The Tibetan cause (the effort to return control—or at least some degree of control—of Tibet to the Tibetans) continues to receive a high degree of international attention. Tibetan organizations (International Campaign for Tibet, Save Tibet Foundation and Free Tibet) and well-organized Tibetans and their supporters, consistently and vigorously advocate for a free, or at

Jared Gange

Young animal herders, early morning, near Saga, Tibet.

Jared Gange

Nomad woman at home on the Tibetan plateau,
15,000 feet above sea level.

least more autonomous, Tibet. Many governments, including the United States, have issued statements critical of China's treatment of Tibetans, pointing to repression of religious activities, closing of monasteries, severe travel restrictions, detention without charges and the ongoing, widespread destruction and replacement of Tibetan homes and structures with Chinese buildings. Sadly, despite these ongoing efforts, Tibet's unique culture and way of life are gradually being snuffed out, and the chances of Tibet regaining even a small measure of self-determination remain close to zero. Areas outside of Tibet, Ladakh (a high mountain region in northern India) and the Tibetan communities in south India, are today more Tibetan than most of Tibet.

Tibetans throughout the world are increasingly concerned with the issue of the successor to the Dalai Lama. The mere existence of a Dalai Lama undermines China's legitimacy as the undisputed government of Tibet and representative of the Tibetan people. The fear, and one that is justified, is that China will prevent the selection of a successor to 83-year-old Tenzin Gyatso, terminating the lineage and thus ending this fundamental, essential tradition.

||||

ANAK DORJE NAMGYAL

TIBET

Anak Dorje was born in a tiny, ancient village in eastern Tibet, in the part of the country known as Kham. Of the twelve children born to his mother, only three survived: two boys and a girl. His father, and his father before him—in fact his male lineage going back hundreds of years—were the village headmen, "Pon," in Tibetan. At a young age, Anak's brother was recognized as a reincarnation of a high lama and sent to a monastery for training in what would become his life's work. Anak was thus in line to take over responsibility for the village after his father.

His village—its name is Gonjo—lies on the gentle, lower slopes of a high mountain. The mountain provides reliable streams for drinking water and crop irrigation. The main crops were barley, wheat, buckwheat and various green vegetables. There was ample pasturage for the family's many yaks, horses, mules, goats and sheep. The farmers' houses, made of rammed earth walls with a log upper story, follow the slope of the hillside, with the village headman's much larger family compound placed at the top (see page 197). This was the setting for Anak's early life, a pre-industrial, almost medieval existence, but peaceful, stable and more or less the norm for the majority of the Tibetan population.

Anak describes the setting:

Many costly wild animals and birds used to roam around freely. Many costly and delicious wild mushrooms and wild green vegetables and specially a root called Yartsa Gunbue, which means "summer grass and winter worm," were so plentiful during summer. This wild root of grass feeds the people of Tibet even today. So that the livelihood of men and animals in Gonjo county used to be one of the best in Tibet.

By 1959, after about 10 years of fighting the Chinese invasion, Tibetan resistance was finally crushed, and the occupation of the country by the Chinese a *fait accompli*. The traditional Tibetan way of life was changed, probably forever, and a massive exodus of Tibetans followed. Tibetans in a position of authority—lamas and their ministers, local leaders and landlords— were likely to be imprisoned by the Chinese or killed on the spot. Thus Anak's father and uncle decided to flee south to India. The hope was that those left behind would not be perceived as a threat by the Chinese and would be allowed to continue their simple farming existence. A further hope was that the invasion would eventually fail, and they, and the many thousands, including the Dalai Lama, who fled Tibet during this time would be able to return to their homes and resume their lives. These hopes were never realized.

Thus, in August of 1959, Anak, aged 15, left Gonjo with his father and uncle and headed toward India. Accompanied by five bodyguards, they left on horseback with a mule train laden with food and supplies,

Anak as a young man with his son.

as well as most of their money and valuables. The most precious cargo was their collection of cherished Buddhist religious items. As they neared the Indian border, they merged with thousands of other Tibetans on the same journey. Perhaps as many as 50,000 had gathered in the vicinity of the town of Penbar, preparing to cross into India. Not surprisingly, this large group was detected by the Chinese, who attacked them with planes and ground troops. Everyone scattered, but many—at least half—of the Tibetans were killed.

Gonjo, Anak's village in Tibet.

Anak's father, mortally wounded, ordered the others to continue without him. Two of their bodyguards were killed, and most of the family's supplies and money lost. Anak, his uncle and the remaining bodyguards struggled onward, now reduced to living off the land, hunting, begging and sometimes stealing from the locals to survive. Anak's group and the families traveling with them now headed north away from the border, making a huge detour north, then west, eventually crossing the desolate Chang Tang Plateau before heading south toward India. Most nights they slept out in the open, even in snow, without a proper tent or adequate clothing. Finally, in the spring of 1961, they crossed into Nepal, and after resting there for some weeks—they lived in a cave and considered it a luxury—arrived in India, in the Uttar Pradesh region. In Anak's words:

> When our group arrived in hotter places like Nepal and India, our clothes started smelling bad, because of never being washed and used constantly for the last two years. At the border of India, the local Indian officer started washing our people's bodies, cut their hair short and neat, fingernails were beautifully trimmed, and they were given food rations and clothing.

In India, Anak and other Tibetan refugees were placed in camps, allowed to adjust to the warmer climate and given food and medical care. In exchange they worked as laborers on road projects. Over the next several years, Anak was able to attend school and learn English and office skills. During this time, the Tibetan Government in Exile, headed by the Dalai Lama and his staff, gradually established itself in the northern Indian town of Dharamsala. After completing his training, Anak enjoyed a successful career with the Tibetan exile government in India.

The Indian government has allocated large tracts of previously uninhabited forest—thousands of acres near the southern city of Mysore—to the Tibetan refugees. Over the years, five major settlements have been established and are today home to about 37,000 Tibetans. While from a farming perspective this area is worlds away from cool, high-elevation Tibet—the livestock and crops have little in common with those of Tibet—these settlements are nevertheless the biggest intact, unfettered Tibetan community in the world, with the possible exception of Indian-controlled Ladakh.

Anak spent his professional career working in south India in rural resettlement projects under the Tibetan-exile government's Department of Home Affairs, based in Dharamsala. He worked with all aspects of the projects, from overseeing the initial clearing of land, to marketing the valuable timber, building houses and administration buildings, working with a Swiss expert on training Tibetans to work with the new crops, assisting with milk production and working with local agricultural cooperatives. In all he spent 28 years working with the resettlement projects, and he has spent a total of 37 years in India.

In 1992 Anak's wife, Tsamchoe Namgyal, won a U.S. visa through the lottery program made possible by the Immigration Act of 1990. This law made available 1,000 expedited visas for Tibetans living in India and Nepal. She and 22 other Tibetans were sent to Burlington, one of 25 designated resettlement sites in the United States. Tsamchoe soon found work as a nurse's aid at Fanny Allen Hospital, where she is still employed. Anak and their children arrived here in 1998, when the families of the lottery winners were allowed to reunite in the U.S. In 2001 they bought a home in South Burlington, and in 2010 Anak retired. Tsamchoe and Anak's five children are now grown. One son is a rinpoche (a high lama) living in Tibet, another an antiquities dealer based in Hong Kong. The third son lives here in Burlington. Their older daughter lives in Gangtok, Sikkim (India), and the younger one lives with her parents in Burlington. Anak, his wife and two of their children are U.S. citizens.

Tsamchoe, Anak's wife, at their home in south India, ca. 1990.

Like most of his compatriots here, Anak and his family have made a success of life in Vermont and outwardly lead a fairly typical American existence in a typical neighborhood. (Ninety percent of the Tibetan families in Vermont own their own homes.) A string of prayer flags arcs across Anak's backyard, and inside his house, as in all Tibetan homes, the family has its Buddhist shrine with pictures of the Dalai Lama, incense, lighted candles and various offerings. Anak spends at least three hours a day with his "routine practices of Dharma." Over the last three years, he has completed eight book-length manuscripts about his life and about Buddhism in Tibet. They are in Tibetan and have not been translated into English.

He describes his present life:

He is kind of a retired person now and loves gardening, to grow all kinds of flowers during summer months, which brings all kinds of beautiful birds, butterflies and bees in his backyard garden. He really loves horses, yaks, cows, sheep, goats, dogs and many more animals, but his home backyard here in Burlington is too small to accommodate all these animals. But yes, he had all these animals in Tibet, which makes him to remember his birthplace every day and night.

Anak has returned to Tibet six times after his escape in 1961: in 1983, 1994, 1995, 2006, 2010 and 2015. He stays in his ancestral home in Gonjo with relatives, for four or five months at a time. His dream is to build a school for the children of his village, as most families refuse to send their kids to the Chinese school, despite being fined for refusing. He is also eager to use his many years' experience working in the settlements in south India to introduce improved varieties of wheat and barley, to introduce better breeding methods for livestock and to carry out much needed tree planting in order to reduce erosion. He is negotiating with the Chinese authorities, but to date little progress has been made.

The Future of Tibet
The Middle Way Approach

The people of Tibet are profoundly religious, and their interpretation of Buddhism and their language, architecture, diet and manner of dress are unique. Isolated and remote, Tibet developed a highly original, stable society of sophistication and complexity. But in 1959, that peaceful isolation ended, and the doors of communist China swung wide open.

It is no surprise that an agrarian, ancient way of life would come under pressure to modernize, but the change in Tibet has come on Chinese terms: Tibet's traditional way of life, particularly its religion, is under assault. There is great sympathy for the Tibetan cause—innumerable proclamations, referendums and protest marches attest to this—and all over the world, close-knit Tibetan communities, including here in Burlington, publicly mark anniversaries, observe religious holidays and travel to important gatherings, especially if the Dalai Lama is present. Members of the exile community born outside of Tibet yearn for a life they have never known, in a place they have never been.

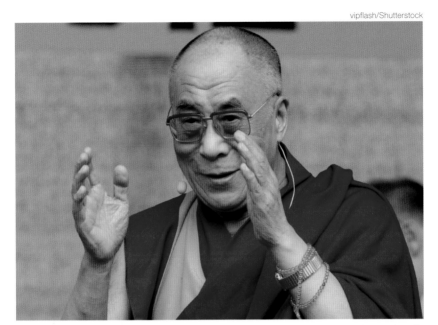

His Holiness the Dalai Lama, the undisputed spiritual leader of the Tibetan people, speaking in Berlin in 2008.

At present, the stated goal for a future Tibet—as laid out by the Dalai Lama and his advisors and accepted by Tibetans throughout the world—is a compromise known as the Middle Way Approach. The idea is to address the two primary issues of disagreement between the Tibetan people and the People's Republic of China such that each side realizes one of its goals and gives in on the other. Thus, Tibetans would no longer demand Chinese acknowledgment Tibet's sovereignty prior to the Chinese takeover; in return, China would grant self-rule to Tibet, albeit as a full-fledged province of China.

The Tibetan Government in Exile describes this solution as "a non-partisan and moderate position that safeguards the vital interests of all concerned parties—for Tibetans, the protection and preservation of their culture, religion and national identity; for the Chinese, the security and territorial integrity of the motherland; and for neighbors and other third parties, peaceful borders and international relations."

China appears to regard the Middle Way Approach as a non-starter, because in their view, Tibet has been a part of China for centuries. Thus the Tibetans' offer to relinquish their claim of independence is an insufficient concession.

201

‖‖‖

GELEK GYATSO PONTSANG

TIBET

Gelek was born on the high plateau of Tibet, in an indescribably beautiful setting, with a 23,500-foot mountain towering over nearby Lake Nam (Nam Tso), at 15,480 feet the highest salt-water lake in the world. Both mountain and lake are sacred to Tibetans and important pilgrimage sites.

Gelek's family were nomads, and they lived in tents of homespun yak hair and tended their livestock of goats, sheep and yaks; food was plentiful. Summers by all accounts were wonderful, with flower-filled meadows and mild temperatures. Winters were tough, but manageable. There was no school available to Gelek, and up until the age of eight, his days were spent playing and taking care of the family's sheep. But about this time, everything changed. Their idyllic existence was upended by the Chinese takeover of Tibet.

In March of 1959, when fighting between the Chinese and Tibetans spread to the capital, Lhasa, the then 24-year-old Dalai Lama, Tibet's spiritual leader, made a hurried escape and fled on horseback to India. The Dalai Lama's flight triggered the exodus of thousands of Tibetans, including Gelek's family. While Gelek's family were nomads, his father was an important local official with the rank of cabinet minister and the Dalai Lama's chief representative for the vast province of Namru, an area roughly the size of New England. For this reason, the Chinese would no doubt have selected him for "corrective" treatment.

Thus Gelek's family, together with many other nomad families (about 1,500 people in all) and their herds of livestock, began what would be a 10-month journey to Nepal. Gelek, being only eight, spent most of the trip tied to a yak, one individual in a veritable sea of humanity and four-leggeds slowly moving south to safety. Traveling with them was a high lama who continually consulted an oracle to keep them on a route safe from Chinese soldiers. Eventually they arrived in the tiny kingdom of Mustang (a protectorate of Nepal) and commenced to suffer through the harshest winter in memory, losing most of their animals. Thrown into extreme poverty, they were forced to sell their valuable jewelry and religious objects in order to buy food.

Gelek's parents, apparently unable to thrive in the lower elevations of Nepal, both died in that first year out of Tibet. His older brother took charge of the family. Other siblings died—Gelek was one of a dozen kids—and the survivors went to work as laborers. Gelek, now 10 years old, and his siblings carried loads of rock to help build the airstrip in nearby Jomsom, in order to earn their daily share of Red Cross food rations.

Dreamstime

From the shore of holy Nam Tso (Lake Nam), where Gelek lived until he was eight.

Yak train carrying salt from Nam Tso, circa 2000.

At one point his older brother sent six of the kids, including Gelek, to Kathmandu on a pilgrimage. It took them two months to make the round trip, walking. They had no money and had to beg for food to survive. In Gelek's words:

> At that time our mind was set on religion, because our father had died, and so many others had died. Before we die we have to go on pilgrimage. No cheating, no fighting, no deceiving other people, just begging. Mind was set on food. Sometimes when you got food you feel good, sometimes they [the locals] would beat you, fine, we just accepted that.

The Tibetans seemed very strange to the local Nepalis. Gelek recalls that even the water buffalos ran from them. After they returned to Jomsom from their pilgrimage, Gelek and his siblings worked on the airport for another year.

Finally, his family was able to settle in one of the Tibetan refugee camps in nearby Pokhara, and Gelek could attend school for the first time in his life. An energetic student, he excelled and graduated from high school at 18. While he had ambitions of becoming a professor, he had no money for university and was, as he says, "blocked."

Jared Gange

Nepalese kids carrying loads, similar to Gelek's experience as a nine-year-old, 1996.

After high school, a chance meeting led to a job in Lumbini (Nepal) as a translator for a high lama. Lumbini is the birthplace of the Buddha, and the city was undergoing the transformation into the major religious and tourist site that it is today. Gelek soon found himself working as a general contractor on building projects. He stayed in Lumbini for 10 years, returning to Mustang in the summer to work as the king's interpreter. The ancient Tibetan community of Mustang, complete with a ruling monarch, lies on the Nepalese–Tibetan border in the Annapurna Region of Nepal. The king died in 2016, and Mustang—one of the most coveted destinations for adventure travelers—has become an administrative district of Nepal.

After their forced exodus from Tibet, many thousands of Tibetans settled in south India, near Mysore, and today there are approximately 37,000 Tibetans living in five communities. In 1979 Gelek moved to one of the resettlement sites, Kollegal, and became involved in milk production and animal husbandry. As the general secretary of the milk producers' co-op, he oversaw all aspects of an operation that produced about 1,000 gallons of milk daily. During this period, he was also an elected representative to the Tibetan Youth Congress, serving two 4-year terms. The Youth Congress is active throughout India and strives to maintain worldwide awareness of the suppression of Tibet. As such, it organizes events protesting the continued refusal of the Chinese authorities to allow Tibet to be governed by Tibetans, for Tibetans.

In 1991, Gelek was one of 1,000 Tibetans to receive a U.S. visa under the American government's visa lottery program for Tibetans living in exile, and he arrived in Burlington June 1, 1993. Family members of lottery winners were initially not given visas. The plan was that they would be allowed to emigrate to the U.S. after two years; however, five years passed before the families were reunited.

Gelek adapted to his new Vermont life and promptly got a job with April Cornell, a clothing and textile importer with strong ties to India. Like many other adult immigrants, in the U.S. he had no choice but to accept a job of much lower status and responsibility than he had held in India. This is a persistent problem for many (adult) immigrants, as work

Willy Cats-Baril

The village of Kagbeni, Mustang, the area in Nepal where Gelek's family first settled after fleeing Tibet. Photo taken 2012.

experience from culturally distant countries, compounded by an imperfect mastery of English, is a profound barrier to a smooth career transition. He remained at April Cornell for 11 years; at one point there were 24 Tibetans employed there.

By working two full-time jobs—at April Cornell and as a dishwasher at Sweetwater's—Gelek was able to take care of his family, buy a car after two years and a house in Burlington's North End after four years. He still lives in the same house with his wife, three of his seven children, three grandchildren and a son-in-law: nine people in all. Two of his three daughters are married to Tibetans. The third, who lives in Minneapolis, married a Mexican man. They speak English together as, not surprisingly, he does not speak Tibetan. In order that their grandchild learn Tibetan, Gelek and his wife offered to have their baby daughter live with them, on the condition that both parents would work full time and save to buy a house. After living in Gelek's home for five years, the little girl speaks fluent Tibetan and is now back in Minneapolis with her parents. As a further instance of cultural and family cohesion, when the parents' work schedule left a gap in child care coverage, Gelek sent one of his sons to Minneapolis to live with them and take care of his little niece.

Gelek Gyatso

Gelek (upper right) with his siblings in Bodhgaya, India, in 2017.

Willy Cats-Baril

The ancient walled city of Lo Manthang, administrative center of the Kingdom of Mustang, on the border of Tibet. Mustang's last king, Jigme Dorje, died in 2016. Gelek and his family escaped from Tibet to safety in Lo Manthang. Photo 2012.

Gelek has worked providing Assisted Living care at Wake Robin Retirement Community in Shelburne as a nurse's aid for 10 years. He describes his attitude toward his job:

> If I put my mind on helping the other person, that frees my mind from stress. If you have to clean up after someone and that person is unable to control themselves, if your mind set is to help, then you are free. In our religion that is the only way to get enlightened: if that person needs help, you have to help them. My parents died when I was very young and I didn't get a chance to serve them. So now I am glad I am able to serve others.

IIIII

TENZIN WASER DHONDUP

INDIA / TIBET

Tenzin was born in northern India, in the foothills of the Himalayan mountains. Like many Tibetans, her parents had fled Chinese-occupied Tibet in 1959 and settled in India, in her mother's case in Gangtok, Sikkim. Her father found his new home in Dharamsala, and that is where they met, married and raised their family. Her father was in the army and later served as a bodyguard to the Dalai Lama. Both of her parents came from a typical, completely self-sufficient setting in rural Tibet. Thus, as was the age-old practice, Tenzin and her three siblings were born at home—in her case, in the kitchen.

A former British hill station, Dharamsala lies high above the fierce heat of the Indian lowlands. Today Dharamsala is the official residence of the Dalai Lama, and it is the seat of the Tibetan Government in Exile. On this steep mountain hillside, thousands of Tibetan refugees and their children have now settled. Many of the refugee children are orphans or have parents too sick or impoverished to care for them. The Tibetan Children's Village (TCV), a network of Tibetan boarding schools based in India, provides an education and a safe, stable upbringing for these, and in fact most, exile Tibetan kids. Tenzin attended TCV, and her parents managed one of the TCV homes, taking care of about 40 kids. After graduating, Tenzin decided she wanted to work in an office, and she moved to Mundgod, in the south of India, to attend secretarial school in the large Tibetan community there.

In 1991, about the time she was finishing her training, a friend informed her that she had won the lottery to go to the USA. Tenzin and about 1,000 other Tibetans—from the exile community in Nepal and India—had been selected through a U.S. Immigration lottery program to receive visas. This news was a surprise for Tenzin, as she had no plans to move to the U.S. and was in fact ambivalent about living here. Unbeknownst to her, her parents had submitted her name to the visa lottery.

However, she quickly warmed to the idea of living in America. After the formalities were completed, Tenzin was sent to Madison, Wisconsin, and, as is typical, began her life in this country living with a sponsor family. Later, in Chicago, she met another Tibetan lottery winner, Sangay Dhondup. On a visit to their parents in India, they married and subsequently moved to Burlington, where Tenzin's best friend from India, also Tibetan, was living. Tenzin has held a variety of jobs here, including 10 years with April Cornell in Williston. For the last 14 years she has worked at the Fletcher Free Library in Burlington.

Jared Gange

Tenzin at home in South Burlington during Losar (Tibetan New Year), with her sons in 2013.

Tenzin's mom, Tsamchoe, serving Tibetan tea and snacks.

Her two sons, now 17 and 19, attend South Burlington High School and Champlain College, respectively. They are fluent in Tibetan, but, as is typical with immigrant families, the kids want to immerse themselves 100% in the new culture, so it's a struggle to keep them speaking Tibetan.

Although Tenzin is well established here—she's a U.S. citizen, she owns a nice house, her kids go off to school every morning and she is happily employed in a public position—in a sense, she lives in a Tibetan bubble and has her whole life. Her social life is Tibetan, and her mother, her sister and her sister's family live with her. To a westerner, her living room would be indistinguishable from the interior of a Tibetan temple. In her response to a question about what she aspires to, Tenzin's thoughts turn to traveling to Tibet, where she has never been.

photos by Katie Figura

Images from the 2019 Losar celebrations in Burlington.

In Tenzin's words:

I want to travel to Tibet. That's my most important place, but it's scary of course. I'm not comfortable going by myself, also with my mom, also because we are female. I would love to take my mom there because her whole family still lives there. This is our country but we are not comfortable with our country. We know our languages, but we are strangers in our own land. It's so sad.

The Chinese government continues to make it almost impossible for non-resident Tibetans to visit Tibet—even if they are American citizens—presumably because of the tense and unpredictable nature of the relationship between Tibetans and the Chinese government. Demonstrations protesting the Chinese occupation of Tibet, and particularly the potential for self-immolations by Tibetans, can occur at any time, especially on anniversaries of important events. Thus Tenzin's trip to her cultural and ancestral homeland, her most important place, remains a dream for the time being.

VIETNAM

n the not too distant past, the United States was fighting a war in Vietnam. Known in the United States as the *Vietnam War*, and in Vietnam as the *American War* or the *Resistance War Against America*, the war cost over 58,000 American lives. Far more Vietnamese lives were lost—approximately 2,000,000 Vietnamese men, women and children died during the war. About 6,000,000 were displaced from their homes, essentially becoming refugees in their own country. Today, 45 years after the American exit from Vietnam, the U.S. and Vietnam enjoy a friendly, productive relationship. Almost half a million American tourists visit Vietnam's vibrant cities and spectacular beaches every year, and many claim Vietnamese food is the best in Southeast Asia. Visitors are impressed by the friendliness of the Vietnamese, despite the death and destruction we brought to their country. While Vietnam is a Communist, one-party state, it's fair to say that tourism and trade considerations are more important aspects of our relationship than our different systems of government.

Vietnam has a long and complex history of wars and foreign dominance involving China, Japan and France. For example, as part of France's Indochina colony, Vietnam, together with Cambodia and Laos, was exploited for its tea, rice, coffee, opium and rubber. However, by 1954 the French had been forced out by Vietnamese nationalist forces. In the ensuing power vacuum, to prevent the communist leader Ho Chi Minh from acquiring control of the country, Vietnam was partitioned into a northern region and a southern region. Led by Ho Chi Minh, communists assumed control of North Vietnam—officially the Democratic Republic of Vietnam—with Hanoi as its capital. In South Vietnam, the United States backed General Diem's pro-Western government—the Republic of South Vietnam—based in Saigon.

Despite the partitioning, hostilities between the North and South continued, and by 1968, South Vietnam, with increasing American involvement, was at war with North Vietnam. The civil war between the North and South is considered a proxy war, as the United States, in supporting the South, was indirectly at war with China, which actively supported the North's war effort. The United States sought to maintain its level of influence, while the Chinese presumably sought to increase theirs.

American soldiers and helicopters in an assault on Viet Cong positions, 1965.

At the time, a widely held theory called the domino effect embodied the notion that if one country in a region were to fall to communist rule, the neighboring countries would succumb as well. This being the height of the Cold War, it was seen as imperative to prevent North Vietnam from winning the conflict, lest Thailand, India and even Australia fall to the communists. Time has shown that the much-discussed domino effect did not play out as feared.

After a costly and ultimately inconclusive engagement—at one point the United States had over 500,000 troops in Vietnam—a cease-fire was negotiated in 1973, and our military returned home. However, the war between the North and South continued until April 30, 1975, when North Vietnam forces captured Saigon and secured control of the entire country. Saigon was subsequently renamed Ho Chi Minh City in honor of North Vietnam's charismatic leader, but "Saigon" is still widely used.

Despite the fact that the war was over, hard times were not over for the Vietnamese people. The victorious northerners inflicted bitter revenge on those who had sided with, or worked for, the Americans. All manner of reprisals, including confiscation of property, "re-education" camps, imprisonment and executions were the order of the day. Extreme food shortages led to mass starvation. With their homes and livelihood taken

Vietnam War protest March on the Pentagon, 1967.

Ho Chi Minh City (Saigon) today, former capital of South Vietnam.

from them, South Vietnamese were forced to live in primitive camps, some of which were located in areas laden with unexploded land mines.

Not surprisingly, hundreds of thousands (ultimately millions) fled or tried to flee the country. "Boat People" became the term to describe Vietnamese who had set off in woefully inadequate boats in a desperate bid to escape the unbearable conditions at home. Over time, the humanitarian crisis in Vietnam benefitted from international attention, and the United States and other nations agreed to admit large numbers of refugees, significantly alleviating the problem.

The number of Vietnamese living in the U.S. is now somewhere between one-and-a-half and two million, most of whom live in Texas and California. San Jose, California, has over 100,000 Vietnamese residents. There are about 1,500 Vietnamese living in the Burlington area, most of whom arrived between 1989 and 2005.

The UNESCO-protected site of Halong Bay showcases Vietnam's incredible scenery.

As the Vietnam War progressed, it became extremely controversial, since it was increasingly seen as a horrific, unjustified waste of lives and resources—on both sides. There were widespread protests, some of them violent: soldiers returning home from 'Nam were abused and spat on, and thousands of draft-age men—"draft dodgers"—fled to Canada rather than serve in the military. The protest movement and erosion of public support for the war were major factors in our withdrawal from Vietnam, two years before the war actually ended. To this day, many Americans, particularly those who served in the military or who lost loved ones, can find no peace, because they are unable to square their service, their sacrifice, with the historical assessment of the war as unnecessary and a disastrous failure.

Surprisingly, the Vietnamese seem to have put the war behind them, at least in casual contacts with Americans. Perhaps this can be attributed to

220

a basic good-naturedness of the Vietnamese people, or perhaps it reflects the considerable economic and financial support provided by overseas Vietnamese living in America. In any event, visitors to Vietnam are amazed by the pleasantness and lack of hostility on the part of the Vietnamese. Officially, the country is old-school communist, with constant, blaring propaganda, a heavily censored press and widespread corruption. The apparent contradiction is that Vietnam is a repressive communist regime, but according to the Vietnam Academy of Social Sciences, "Vietnam's development goal by 2020 is to become a modern industrialized country of middle income."

EMMY TRAN

VIETNAM

Emmy, her parents and two sisters arrived in Burlington from Vietnam via the Philippines in 1993. From their home in Burlington's North End, 16-year-old Emmy was able to walk to Burlington High School, and her parents could take the bus to their custodial night shift jobs at UVM. Today, more than 20 years later, Emmy runs a successful hair salon, and she owns her home in Williston and a rental property in Winooski. She has three sons. Her oldest, Phillip, is a sophomore at UVM, studying computer science; her middle son, Anthony, is a sophomore at Champlain Valley Union High School; and her youngest, Jaden, aged seven, goes to Williston Elementary School. All are excellent students.

Emmy was born in South Vietnam, in her mother's hometown, Long Khanh, about one and a half hours' drive from Ho Chi Minh City (formerly Saigon). When Emmy was born, in 1977, the Vietnam War had ended just two years earlier, and reprisals and executions by the Viet Cong and North Vietnamese were still taking place.

During the war, Bien Hoa, a major city near Emmy's hometown, was home to a large American base. As the war drew to a close, the area was the scene of intense fighting. After the war, because there had been a large American presence there, and because of the largely pro-American

Dreamstime

Life as a street vendor is not easy.

population, this part of Vietnam was a focus of the victorious communist government's contempt and abuse for years. If we think of the Vietnam War as a civil war between the North and South, not only did the South lose, but it was—and is today—occupied by its former opponent, the communist North. Thus, like hundreds of thousands—perhaps millions—of South Vietnamese families, Emmy's family lost their house and livelihood. In fact, they lost pretty much everything.

Her mother was reduced to working as a street vendor in order to put food on the table. Because the communist regime was opposed to private enterprise, and because of her inability to pay the punishingly high taxes imposed on her meager earnings—and still provide for her family—she was arrested and sent to prison for three years.

While her mom was in prison, Emmy's father struggled to make ends meet by working as a street photographer taking portraits. However, since he had worked with the Americans, the family was under scrutiny from the authorities and never felt safe. Emmy's uncle, her mom's brother, was a barber and had made his living cutting hair for American soldiers. One day he was taken away for questioning, never to be seen again. These circumstances, shared by so many South Vietnamese, were grounds for applying for refugee status. In 1992, after eight years of waiting, Emmy's family was finally given the green light to emigrate to America. In their case, her family's application was looked upon favorably by U.S. immigration officials because her parents had adopted a child fathered by an American: the child's mother was so desperately poor she couldn't support her.

Emmy's parents were indescribably happy when they received the good news. The family was transferred to one of the refugee centers in the Philippines for further processing and given a chance to learn English. After six months in the transition camp, they were sent to the U.S., to Burlington.

Thus, at age 16, knowing very little English and unfamiliar with America, Emmy found herself a student at Burlington High School. School was a struggle at first, but she and her younger sister persevered and graduated. Her sister went on to graduate from UVM. After graduating from high school in 1997, Emmy married and had her first child the next year. But, determined to be self-sufficient and own her own business, she attended Vermont Cosmetology School and trained to be a hair stylist.

Emmy Tran

Emmy's three boys, Christmas 2017.

The building in Vietnam that Emmy's parents bought for their relatives still living in Vietnam.

Today, with her hair salon well established, Emmy's main focus is on raising her three children. Now divorced, she is the children's main provider, and all three boys live with her. She sees her two sisters, both of whom live in California, less than she used to: everyone is busy with their work and their families. Her best friend from high school, also Vietnamese, lives in Florida, and the two of them get together whenever possible.

Emmy has had employees in the past, but she finds it easier these days to run the salon herself. She is booked from morning to evening, five days a week. In Emmy's words:

> I am so comfortable in my job. Most of my clients I know them before they get married. Now I know their kids. They are friends. I really love, love my job.

In the 21 years that she has lived here, Emmy has been back to Vietnam three times; her last visit was eight years ago. The country is rife with corruption and she finds being there very stressful. She also feels the food is not particularly safe because of the widespread use of chemicals.

Emmy's father, now 75, retired a few years ago, but her mother still works full-time, in fact she continues to work two full shifts, one at St. Michael's College and one at UVM. She often works 80 hours a week. Neither parent has learned much English, just enough to get by. When they arrived in Vermont they were penniless, in fact they were in debt to the U.S. government. After three years they had paid back the costs associated with moving them to the U.S.; and they were able to begin saving. Over the years her parents have been able to send enough money to their relatives in Vietnam to make a huge difference in their lives, lifting them out of poverty and enabling them to become successful business people.

Emmy's comments on life in Vietnam today:

> The people who have connections get richer. Those that don't, get poorer. For most people there is no future in Vietnam. If I lived there, I would probably be a street vendor, like my mom. You have to pay most of your earnings in taxes. How can you survive with the money left over? If you get into difficulty here, we have welfare and other social programs to help you. There you die. Every single day, I'm telling you, I am thankful to be here.

LAN HONG

VIETNAM

Lan was born in Saigon, the capital of South Vietnam. The period of French colonization of Indochina—Indochina covered the area of present-day Vietnam, Laos, and Cambodia—had ended in 1954, and when Lan was born, in 1958, Vietnam consisted of two distinct political regions, the communist North and the western-oriented South.

Lan's father drove a taxi and her mother sold vegetables in the local market. Lan's early life was spent in Saigon; she started school at age 5 and continued until she was 15. Lan is the second oldest of four sisters, two of whom still live in Vietnam. Her third sister lives here in Burlington and works in Lan's restaurant.

In 1975, after the conquest and occupation of South Vietnam by North Vietnamese forces—the Viet Cong and the North Vietnamese Army— times were very tough for South Vietnamese like Lan and her family. The animosity between South and North Vietnamese was intensified by South Vietnam's intimate relationship with the U.S. military during the Vietnam War. From the North Vietnamese perspective, their southern countrymen represented the enemy: they *were* in fact the enemy. Since the American war effort was based in South Vietnam, many thousands of Vietnamese worked for and with the Americans during the conflict. As a result, when the

Jared Gange

Lan's two older daughters, Jade and Thao, both work in the family restaurant, 2018.

North took over the South, South Vietnamese found themselves in grave danger. Homes, businesses, property and financial assets were confiscated. All manner of reprisals took place: thousands of South Vietnamese were executed. Lan's family lost their savings and had almost no money for food and none for schooling. Her parents had separated, and Lan, her mother and her sisters struggled desperately to make ends meet.

The Viet Cong appropriated Lan's house, and her family, like many southern families, was sent to work on a farm. To help alleviate the food crisis in the years after the war, the Viet Cong initiated a program whereby thousands of southerners were forced to relocate to war-ravaged or previously uncultivated areas, in mountainous or jungle terrain, to start farms in order to increase food production. Lan's family was assigned to Chien Khu D, "War Zone D," notorious for its high concentration of unexploded bombs and mines. Loss of life or limbs was commonplace. In Lan's words, *Every day I hear boom.* Their food was mostly sweet potatoes, with no tea or rice. Drinking water was collected from roof runoff. Again in Lan's words: *You get nothing in the jungle, just sad people everywhere.*

After three years of this harsh existence, the Viet Cong abandoned the forced-farming program, and Lan's mother and sisters were able to return to Saigon. But having lost their house, they were forced to live on the street and were barely able to survive. Their situation eventually improved when they were able to move in with Lan's older sister and her husband.

Later on, after Lan married, she and her husband moved to the coastal city of Kien Giang to live with her husband's family. The following years passed relatively uneventfully and Lan gave birth to three girls. Lan's sister-in-law had married an American soldier before the war and given birth to a son. When her husband returned to America at the end of the war, the child remained in Vietnam and was cared for by Lan's mother-in-law. It turned out to be fortuitous that the family had a child whose father was American.

In 1989, the Viet Cong (pronounced *yee camg* in Vietnamese) offered them, and other families with children of American fathers, a proposal: Take their half-American child out of Vietnam, and other family members would be allowed to leave the country as well. Thus, after two years of waiting, the American authorities granted Lan, her husband and their three

Lan and her three daughters on their way to the U.S. Refugee Processing Center, Bataan, Philippines, 1993.

daughters, as well as the baby's mother, permission to emigrate to America.

Their first stop was the Philippine Refugee Processing Center, a camp and staging area for Indochinese refugees destined for the U.S. The camp was located on the Bataan Peninsula (outside Manila) near Subic Bay, then the site of a large U.S. naval base. There they lived for six months. Although pictures of the camp make it look pleasant enough, according to Lan, *These were scary times, killing almost every day.* This was partly due to the settling of scores among the refugees. During this waiting period, Lan taught elderly Vietnamese how to read and write, and her husband assumed the role of leader for their group of refugees, helping with the distribution of food rations.

With almost no possessions, and unaware of our winter weather, they arrived in Burlington in February, completely unprepared for the bitter cold, snow and ice. Rounding out their rough start, their assigned apartment was drafty, dirty and overrun with mice and cockroaches. Upon their arrival,

Jared Gange

Traditional offerings to the gods, Vietnamese New Year, at Lan's restaurant.

they received a 20-pound bag of rice and a bottle of fish sauce, but nothing else, not even cooking utensils. Fortunately, a Vietnamese family living in the same building helped them settle in.

Three months into their stay here, police paid Lan a visit to inquire why her children weren't attending school. With the help of an interpreter, she was able to explain her situation, obtain a more helpful sponsor and to get her girls started in school. After a year and a half in their sub-standard apartment, Lan was able to secure a decent apartment for her family.

Today, after years of hard work, she owns the very popular Pho Hong restaurant in Burlington's North End. Lan works 6 days a week, 12 hours a day, often until midnight. On their busy days—Friday, Saturday and Sunday—five people work in the tiny kitchen and three wait on tables. Even on a slow night, it's best to get there early to avoid a wait.

When Lan arrived in Burlington, she first took a job making tomato sauce. Later she worked as a housekeeper at the Radisson, then as a janitor at UVM. Finally, after a stint at a local Thai restaurant, she was ready to start a restaurant of her own.

Lan visits her mother in Vietnam periodically. Her mother has never been to America and has no desire to visit. She says it's too long a trip for her and too foreign a place. She has a good life in Vietnam, thanks in large part to the financial support Lan is able to provide.

While Lan misses Saigon, and especially the way things were before the war, she finds the current government corrupt and hard to deal with. She describes arriving at the airport on a recent visit:

> When I give them my passport, if there is no money in there, the official will say something like: 'Oh, something is wrong with your passport, your papers, go over there and wait.' I understand, so I put ten dollars in my passport and suddenly everything is okay.

Her oldest daughter Jade, 37, lives in the North End; Thao, 35, lives in Winooski. Her third daughter, a UVM graduate, is attending nursing school in Baltimore. Her son, now 17, was born here. Lan has four grandchildren, two each from her two older daughters. Lan has lived here 25 years and has no plans to leave:

> Too cold, but I like it. I have a job, I have food, money, everything what I need. If we stayed in Vietnam, we dead.

GLOSSARY

AALV – Association of Africans Living in Vermont, provides training, counseling and guidance to refugees of all nationalities in the Burlington area.

The American Dream – the belief that in America, success, prosperity and even wealth can be achieved by anyone willing to work hard, and that one's social class and country of origin are not determiners of future success.

apartheid – policy of separation and legalized discrimination, from the South African/Afrikaans word meaning "apartness."

Arab Spring – period of pro-democracy protests, starting in Tunisia in 2010, that spread throughout much of the Middle East.

assimilation – adaptation to and integration into, a culture different from the culture of one's birth.

asylum – the granting of protection from persecution; implies having moved to another country for safety.

Bantu – individuals from central Africa—and their descendants—who settled in northern African areas, such as those moving from Tanzania to Somalia.

BDS – Boycott, Divestment and Sanctions is a global campaign that promotes *boycotts* of Israeli products, lobbies for *divestment* from Israeli projects and companies and argues for *sanctions* against Israel to force Israel to grant equal rights to its Palestinian citizens and to respect Palestinian property.

Black Hawk Down – two-day battle in Mogadishu, Somalia, in October 1993, between predominantly American forces and local militia, triggered by the botched kidnapping of two Somali officials by American forces. Two Black Hawk helicopters were shot down during the battle.

Bosniak – Bosnian individual who is Muslim, as distinct from such non-Muslim Bosnian citizens as Serbs and Croats.

Buddhist – person adhering to the Buddhist religion, a follower of the teachings of Buddha. Practiced in Tibet, Thailand, Japan, China, Mongolia and other countries.

burka – loose-fitting, body-length garment covering one's entire body from head to toe, worn in public by conservative Muslim women.

caste – individual's position in a structured social hierarchy, all-important for Hindus. Determines social status, marriage options and career opportunities.

checkpoint – point of control, usually on a road, where passage is monitored and controlled by police or military.

conflict minerals – minerals extracted from areas embroiled in conflict; for example, gold, cobalt and diamonds from the DR Congo.

Croat – member of an ethnic group in Croatia, Bosnia and Slovenia professing the Catholic faith.

Dalai Lama – spiritual leader of Tibetan Buddhists; the current reincarnation in the centuries' old series of previous incarnate Dalai Lamas.

Dayton Accords – peace agreement ending the Bosnian War. Terms of the agreement were negotiated in Dayton, Ohio, in 1995.

deportation – lawful expulsion of a person from a country.

diaspora – virtual community of members of an ethnic or national group residing outside their country, or countries, of origin. Examples include the Palestinian diaspora and the Russian diaspora.

Dinka – major clan of South Sudan, a traditional cattle-herding culture.

ethnic group – group sharing common religion, language or culture.

first generation – the first generation of a family born in a given country; for example, children whose parents were refugees.

Gaza – self-governing city of two million Palestinians on Israel's Mediterranean coast, under Israeli army control. Also referred to as the Gaza Strip.

genocide – act of, or intention to, exterminate an entire group of people based on ethnicity, country of origin, religion or ideology.

genocidaire – active participant (belligerent) in the 1994 Rwandan Genocide.

green card – document giving non-U.S. citizens the right to work and reside in the United States.

halal – food, especially meat, that Muslims are permitted to consume, according to the dictates of the Koran.

hijab – head covering, a scarf, worn in public by Muslim women.

Hindu – person practicing the Hindu religion, adjective for same.

Hutu – largest ethnic group of Rwanda, making up about 85% of the population.

IDP – internally displaced person, one who has been forced to relocate within her or his home country. Usually conflict-related, but drought, famine and ethnic persecution are also factors.

illegal settlement – in the context of Israeli–Palestinian relations, denotes the construction of homes and villages by Jewish settlers in the West Bank, on Palestinian-owned land.

Islam – religion of Muslims, based on Muhammed's teachings received from Allah, and transcribed in book form, the Koran.

Islamic State – insurgent, militant group known as ISIS or Daesh whose avowed goal is to establish a Muslim state based on a conservative interpretation of the Koran.

Jhapa – region in southeastern Nepal, site of refugee camps for expelled Bhutanese of Nepali origin.

jihad – holy war in Islamic context.

kleptocracy – governance based on plundering a country's resources and wealth by the country's officials.

Latino – person with cultural ties to Latin America, especially Mexico and Central America.

Lhotshampa – ethnic Nepalis living in Bhutan, most of whose ancestors migrated to Bhutan at the invitation of the Bhutanese government.

Lost Boys of Sudan – young boys, and some girls, rendered homeless by civil war who walked hundreds of miles—over a period of years—from their homes in southern Sudan to Ethiopia and later to refugee camps in Kenya.

migrant worker – laborer, typically a farmer worker, who has moved temporarily from another country—from Mexico to the United States, for example—for the express purpose of finding employment.

mosque – Muslim place of worship.

naturalization – process of adopting the citizenship of another country.

Palestine – geographic region on the eastern shore of the Mediterranean, of historical and religious importance to Muslims, Jews and Christians—territory now comprising the State of Israel.

Perestroika – period of economic restructuring and reform in the Soviet Union, that led to the breakup of the USSR.

refugee – person forced to leave his or her home country, for reasons of conflict, drought, famine, religious persecution, or the like.

refugee camp – living area for refugees—usually in a neighboring country—providing minimal levels of security, housing, food, health services and education.

repatriation – in the refugee context, return to one's home country.

resettlement – in the refugee context, permanent relocation in a new country, with an implied path to citizenship.

Serb – member of one of the three major ethnic groups in the Balkans, usually adhering to the Eastern Orthodox religion, politically loyal to Serbia.

Shia – minority sect of Islam, comprising approximately 15% of Muslims worldwide.

Somali Bantu – Somali individual with Central African roots.

Somali Somali – Somali individual with Arab roots.

Sufism – mystical sect of Islam, official religion of Senegal.

Sunni – majority sect of Islam, comprising 80% to 90% of Muslims worldwide. Practiced in Egypt, Saudi Arabia, Syria, India, Indonesia, Turkey and many other countries.

Swahili – language spoken throughout Tanzania, Congo, Kenya, Uganda and South Africa. The native tongue of about 5 million speakers, but a second language for over 100 million. Language of trade and international communication, the *lingua franca* of the region.

Tutsi – minority ethnic group in Rwanda, making up about 15% of the population, persecuted during the Rwandan Genocide.

UNHCR – United Nations High Commissioner for Refugees, a major humanitarian organization; also known as the UN Refugee Agency.

USCRI – U.S. Committee for Refugees and Immigrants. Protects the rights and addresses the needs of persons in forced or voluntary migration worldwide and supports their transition to a normal life.

visa – document giving formal permission to enter a foreign country.

VRRP – Vermont Refugee Resettlement Program, now renamed USCRI Vermont. Based in Colchester, receives newly arriving refugees and facilitates transition to life here. Upon arrival, VRRP provides initial housing, food, money and interpreter services.

West Bank – contested eastern region of Israel, lying west of the Jordan River and the Dead Sea. Palestinian-occupied for hundreds of years, but steeped in Jewish history and the location of Jewish holy sites, captured by Israel in the Six-Day War in 1967.

Zionism – European movement advocating the creation of a Jewish homeland; the driving force behind the establishment of the state of Israel.

REFERENCES
Selected Titles

A Time for Machetes: *The Rwandan Genocide: The Killers Speak.* Jean Hatzfeld. English translation, 2005. Brief history of the genocide with chilling accounts by imprisoned Hutu killers of the methodical, unemotional way they went about killing their Tutsi teachers, neighbors and friends.

Balkan Ghosts*: A Journey Through History.* Robert Kaplan, 1993. Travelogue and history of the Balkans, written before the Bosnian War. Includes assorted postwar opinion pieces by the author.

Beyond the Sky and the Earth: *A Journey into Bhutan.* Jamie Zeppa, 2000. A young Canadian's account of living and teaching in Bhutan with some discussion of the deepening cultural rifts that ultimately led to the expulsion of over 100,000 Bhutanese of Nepali ancestry.

Black Lamb and Grey Falcon*: A Journey Through Yugoslavia.* Rebecca West, 1941. Classic account of a journey in the Balkans, immediately prior to World War II. Considered a masterpiece of travel writing.

Bosnia*: A Short History.* Noel Malcom, 1994. History of Bosnia from the medieval period into the first years of the Bosnian War.

Bosnia & Hercegovina*: A Tradition Betrayed.* Donia and Fine, 1994. Covers the medieval and Ottoman history of the region and the Bosnian War up to 1994.

Congo*: The Epic History of a People.* David van Reybrouck, 2014 (English edition). Comprehensive, authoritative history of the Democratic Republic of Congo.

Dispatches. Michael Herr, 1977. Based in Saigon during the Vietnam War, author spent a year in Vietnam and was present at the Battle of Hué. Considered one of the best books on the Vietnam War and a classic of war reporting.

Displaced: *My Journey and Stories from Refugee Girls Around the World.* Malala Yousafzai, 2019. Malala's story and the refugee experiences of twelve girls from various countries.

Frontiers of Heaven: *A Journey to the End of China.* Stewart, 2004. Award-winning account of a lengthy, thoughtful journey across China, from Shanghai to Xian to Turfan to Kashgar.

God Grew Tired of Us. John Bul Dau, Published 2007. Life story of a Lost Boy of Sudan. Has been made into a documentary of the same name.

In Exile from the Land of Snows: *The first full account of the Dalai Lama and Tibet since the Chinese Conquest.* John Avedon, 1984.

In the Footsteps of Mr. Kurtz: *Living on the Brink of Disaster in Mobutu's Congo.* Michela Wrong, 2001. Well-researched account of Mobutu's 32-year dictatorial rule of Zaire, known today as the Democratic Republic of Congo.

My Promised Land: *The Triumph and Tragedy of Israel.* Ari Shavit, 2013. Award-winning, readable history of Israel and Zionism by an Israeli historian. but lacks adequate detail on the Palestinian experience.

Our Harsh Logic. *Israeli Soldiers' Testimonies from the Occupied Territories, 2000–2010.* Published in 2012. Compilation of hundreds of accounts by Israeli soldiers of the Israeli Defense Force's (the Israeli army) harsh treatment and systemic violence towards Palestinian residents in the West Bank and Gaza.

Secret Tibet. Fosco Maraini, 2000. Comprehensive, well-illustrated treatment of the cultural and religious history of Tibet.

Seven Years in Tibet. Heinrich Harrer, 1953. Adventure of two Austrian mountaineers, one of whom became a tutor the teenage Dalai Lama. Made into a film of the same name, starring Brad Pitt.

The Battle of Mogadishu: *Firsthand Accounts From the Men of Task Force Ranger.* Edited by Eversmann and Schilling, 2004. Story of Black Hawk Down, a daring raid by Army Rangers in the Somali capital. The humiliating failure of the raid had far-reaching consequences for America's policy in Africa.

The Ethnic Cleansing of Palestine. Ilan Pappe, 2006. An Israeli historian's well-documented, forceful account sheds new light on the Palestinians' expulsion from their homes and villages in the period leading up to, and after, the creation of the state of Israel in 1948.

we wish to inform you that tomorrow we will be killed with our families: *Stories from Rwanda.* Philip Gourevitch, 1998. First-person account of post-genocide Rwanda by an American journalist.

REFUGEE ARRIVALS IN VERMONT
1989 through June 2019

Number of refugees by country, and by region, with arrival years
for countries with 10 or more total refugee arrivals

Burundi	2004–2009	125
Congo–Brazzaville	2000–2007	144
Democratic Republic of Congo	2005–2019	366
Rwanda	2005–2006	11
Somalia	2003–2010 and 2013–2017	839
Sudan	2001–2009	154
Togo	2001–2005	26
Bosnia	1993–2004	1710
Kosovo	1999	58
Azerbaijan	2003–2004	34
Russia	2005–2008	99
Uzbekistan	2005–2006	55
Other former Soviet Union countries	1995–1997	25
Afghanistan	1999, 2001–2002	32
Iran	1998, 2016	11
Iraq	2008–2017	280
Syria	2018	14
Bhutan	2008–2018	2066
Burma	2008–2018	317
Vietnam	1989–2002	1056

The above list of refugee resettlement totals from 20 countries, out of a
total of 38 countries, comprises about 93% of the total number of refugees
resettled in Vermont in the period 1989 through June 2019. Four countries,
Bhutan, Bosnia, Somalia and Vietnam, make up 71% of the total.

Data supplied by U.S. Committee for Refugees and Immigrants Vermont (formerly VRRP).

ACKNOWLEDGMENTS
and Sponsors

Suddenly You Are Nobody owes its existence to the individuals who were willing to sit through long interviews—two, three, sometimes four sessions—while a person from a different culture tried to develop an understanding of the most basic aspects of their previous lives, and then followed with probing questions about events best forgotten. Despite this, most participants were enthusiastic, even impatient, to get their stories "out there," because they know their countries of origin and their cultures are a complete mystery to many of us. Unknown, and thus easy to ignore or to fear, they are diminished. This book, and the discussions it will generate, aims to validate these New Americans, their backgrounds and their traditions.

The 153 photos in the book come from sources and photographers from all over the world. Some of the photos were made available at no charge, some were taken by the author and others were purchased.

Photographer Katie Figura donated her time for many photo shoots—often on very short notice. Her rapport with her subjects is evident in the portraits she has created for this book. Likewise, photographer David Seaver was generous with his time and talent on several photo shoots. Tuva Bogsnes, media director of the Norwegian Refugee Council, granted the project access to the NRC's photo archive, making available photos which would otherwise be extremely difficult to obtain, for example, the book's cover photos, as well as the images from Somalia and South Sudan.

The excellent series of articles on New Americans who have settled in our area, written by *Seven Days* reporter Kymelya Sari, were a source of both inspiration and information. Pamela Polston and Don Eggert of *Seven Days* magazine generously allowed the use of photos from Kymelya's articles, taken by staff photographers Eva Sollberger and Matt Thorsen.

Without the interpreting help from Pemba Sherpa (Nepali), Mohamed "Mike" Kalil (Arabic) and Marcela Pino (Spanish), the resulting stories would have been incomplete and inaccurate. In particular, Marcela's help in understanding Alberto's story, and the dramatic and unexpected turn it took, was absolutely essential.

Suddenly You Are Nobody was designed and "built" by Andrea Gray. She has been involved from the beginning and has patiently tolerated its many twists and turns, not to mention the inefficient, annoying "why don't you design it and lay it out as I write it" approach imposed on her by the author. Copy editor Connie Day found a shocking number of punctuation and grammar misssteps: grateful for that!

Some of the individuals profiled in the book were able to go beyond their own stories and shed light on the larger context pertinent to their particular histories. This was especially true of the contributors from Bosnia (Slavojka Avdibegovic, Adna Karabegovic, Alma Mujezinovic), Bhutan (Bidur Dahal and Rita Neophany), Palestine (Wafic Faour), Russia (Val Kagan), South Sudan (Peter Deng) and Tibet (Gelek Gyatso and Anak Dorje).

Michelle Jenness and Rita Neophany of AALV (Association of Africans Living in Vermont) gave excellent advice and provided suggestions for possible subjects to interview.

Pablo Bose, professor in University of Vermont's Geography Department, took the time to read the manuscript and suggested several improvements.

Julia Alvarez kindly agreed to write the book's foreword, for which I am very grateful. Professor Alvarez is a prolific author and is internationally known for her autobiographical novel, *How the García Girls Lost Their Accents* and, *In the Time of the Butterflies*, the tragic story of four sisters in the Dominican Republic during Trujillo's brutal dictatorship.

Financial sponsors are George W. Mergens Foundation and Betsy Austin.

ABOUT THIS BOOK

*S*uddenly You Are Nobody is an overview of recently arrived refugees and immigrants to Vermont—primarily to the greater Burlington area—from the early 1990s to the present. The compelling life stories of thirty men and women, from seventeen countries, inform us about the circumstances that cause people to leave their homes and their countries, in many cases after having lost everything—house, belongings, even family members—and what it is like to begin anew in a country where no one speaks your language, or enjoys the same food you do, or knows little to nothing about your country and why you fled.

Countries with a larger refugee presence here—Bosnia, Bhutan, Somalia and Vietnam—have, in general, more subjects profiled in this book than do the less numerous groups. Some countries with very few residents here, for example Syria and Iraq, are represented as well, because of the large number of refugees worldwide from these countries. Rounding out the picture of recent arrivals, a number of immigrants, who are not refugees, are included in the book as well.

In addition to the individual stories, most of the countries represented in the book are described in separate introductory segments. These segments immediately precede the individual stories from that country. If an individual profiled in the book is an immigrant, then his or her country does not have an introductory segment. In the case of Iraq and Syria, two countries with large refugee populations, relevant country information is included with their respective individual's histories.

As most of the subjects interviewed for this book are from Burlington and adjoining towns, readers from the area will be familiar with the towns and locations mentioned. Readers from other areas in Vermont, and from outside Vermont, may assume that the town names mentioned are in Vermont and near Burlington, unless otherwise stated.

Writing and researching this book has been a part-time endeavor: the first interviews were done six years ago. During that span of time, as with any group of people, several subjects have moved away, a few have gotten married or divorced and one has passed away—still others were just arriving in this country. During these six years circumstances have improved in some countries and worsened in others, and sadly, new crises have arisen, for example the expulsion of hundreds of thousands of Rohingya muslims from Myanmar and the ongoing destruction of Syria.

Suddenly You Are Nobody is intended for the general audience, but the hope is that students and their teachers, both at the high school and college level, will find it interesting and useful as well. While there are a number of books on the refugee experience—Malala has recently published a book in the U.K. based on stories of 12 refugee women; a book has been written about the Somali community in Lewiston, Maine; and a book similar to this one was published in Norway a few years ago. But up until now there has been little or nothing available in this country that provides, through an informative and sympathetic account of the backgrounds of recent refugee and immigrant arrivals, a path to understanding how fundamentally similar we are, whether we are from Bosnia or Burlington, Vershire or Vietnam, Tibet or Ticonderoga. This realization reduces fear and distrust and paves the way for a more productive and harmonious co-existence for all. Of course, there are differences between cultures: food, language, religion and social norms, to name a few. But rather than letting these differences frighten us, let's allow them to inform and enlighten us about the richness and variety of human experience.